Transactions
of the
American Philosophical Society
Held at Philadelphia
For Promoting Useful Knowledge
Vol. 87, Pt. 6

John Ogden,
Abolitionist and Leader
in Southern Education

DENNIS K. MCDANIEL
Curator of Community and Domestic Life
The State Museum of Pennsylvania

American Philosophical Society
Independence Square • Philadelphia
1997

Copyright © 1997 by the American Philosophical Society for its *Transactions* series. All rights reserved.

ISBN:0-87169-876-5
US ISSN: 0065-9746

Library of Congress Cataloging-in-Publication Data

McDaniel, Dennis K., 1936-
　John Ogden, abolitionist and leader in southern education / Dennis K. McDaniel.
　　p.　cm. -- (Transactions of the American Philosophical Society, ISSN 0065-9746 ; vol. 87, pt. 6)
　Includes bibliographical references and index.
　ISBN 0-87169-876-5
　1. Ogden, John, 1824-1910. 2. Fisk University--Presidents--Biography. 3. College presidents--Tennessee--Biography. I. Title. II. Series: Transactions of the American Philosophical Society ; v. 87, pt. 6.
LC2851.F5170436　1997
370'.92--dc21
[B]　　　　　　　　　　　　　　　　　　　　　　　　97-42359
　　　　　　　　　　　　　　　　　　　　　　　　　　　　CIP

Contents

Preface v
Chronology vii
Introduction 1
Chapter 1. Early Life in the Buckeye State and Midwestern
    Beginnings of a Normal School Career 3
Chapter 2. Civil War Interruptions: Lieutenant Ogden and the
    First Wisconsin Cavalry 11
Chapter 3. Right Back South: Freedmen's Bureau Educator in
    Tennessee and Kentucky 24
Chapter 4. Establishing Fisk in 1865 and Leading It as School
    and University 32
Chapter 5. Students, Chapels, and Churches 51
Chapter 6. Leaving Nashville, 1870 74
Chapter 7. Some Good Years, Some Bleak Years: Later Work in
    Ohio, Washington, D.C., and North Dakota 86
Chapter 8. Retirement and Old Age in Minnesota and
    Washington State 93
Appendix I: Selected Poems 95
Appendix II: Ogden flyers 103
Appendix III: Inaugural Address of John Ogden, A.M. Given
    at the State Normal School, Winona, Minnesota 106
Bibliography 128
Index 132

Illustrations

1. Flyer for John Ogden talk, McNeely Normal School, Hopedale, Ohio, 1856.   5
2. "The Pursuit of Knowledge under Difficulties," artist's depiction of Lt. John Ogden and Lt. George W. Kirkpatrick attempting to read a road sign at night in South Carolina during escape attempt, December 1864.
3. "Recaptured," artist's depiction of Ogden and Kirkpatrick treed by dogs and captured, near Edgefield, S.C.
4. Fisk School (later University), opened 1866 in former Army Hospital buildings in central Nashville.
5. John Ogden, *ca.* 1900.
6. John Ogden's second wife, Anna Brewster Ogden (1842-1908), *ca.* 1858.

Preface

Who was John Ogden, the first Superintendent—later Principal and President—of Fisk School, today's Fisk University? Was he, as some contemporaries said—and certain scholars have casually written—Dr. Ogden? A Methodist minister? An educator from Pennsylvania? An ex-Army Captain? A veteran of the Civil War from the Second Wisconsin Cavalry Regiment? A moral threat to female students? A despiser of blacks? A man not interested in church building? No; all these terms of address and descriptions are incorrect—but they provide hints about where and how Ogden did spend his life, what interested him, and how he was the subject of inaccurate, scurrilous gossip, and the subject of inaccurate, respectful addresses.

Some years ago I was associated with an institution, then known as G.A.R. Memorial Hall Museum, in the State Capitol in Madison (today the Wisconsin Veterans Museum), which owned a barely legible unpublished manuscript in John Ogden's hand. Tracking down who he was and what he had done led from one thing to another, including many archival repositories, helpful staffs, interested scholars, and even Ogden descendants—though it took a decade to find them. Among the things that turned up were the contradictions above. Part of the purpose of this book is to correct all these misapprehensions, incorrect titles, and scurrilities. The larger purposes I try to explain in the Introduction.

Many people have helped during these years. I want especially to thank John Ogden's great-granddaughter, Arden Grenfell of Kirkland, Washington, and her late husband, Dave (sic) Ogden Larimer John Ogden's great-grandson, but with a different grandmother. They provided many documents and photos. Helen Williams of Seattle, another of John Ogden's great-granddaughters, also assisted with documents. One of John Ogden's grandsons, the late Don Larimer of Portland, Oregon, showed me papers and recounted his own family traditions. A lady with a tenacious memory, Ms. Carolyn A. Davis, of the George Arents Research Library at Syracuse University, led me to George Fox College in Newberg, Oregon, and Mr. Merrill Johnson who led me to the family. Dr. Clifton Johnson, then Director, Amistad Research Center, led me originally to Ms. Davis and was particularly kind in other ways.

Beginning at the beginning, I owe thanks to Ms. Pauline Reindl of the Crestline (Ohio) Historical Society, Ms. Nancy Pryor of the Washington-Northwest Room, Washington State Library in Olympia; to John H. Reed, Ohio Wesleyan University Archives; to Miss Lillian Skeele, Worthington (Ohio) Historical Society; to Barney Dunbar Lamar, III, and his cousin, Charles Black Hammond, both of Augusta, Georgia; to Maxime LaFantasie of the Fales Library, New York University; to Lynne Wolfe, Mark D. Van Ells, and Richard Zeitlin of the Wisconsin Veterans Museum; to Ms. Jami Peelle, Special Collections Librarian at Kenyon College; and to Roger Frazier, Fulton County Historical Society, Wauseon, Ohio.

Besides these specially helpful people, some institutions deserve to be recognized for the general assistance they have rendered on many occasions: the Amistad Research Center, the Tennessee State Library and Archives, the State Library of Pennsylvania, the State Museum of Pennsylvania Library, the Library of Congress, the National Archives, Van Pelt Library at the University of Pennsylvania, the Washingtoniana Room of the Martin Luther King Library in Washington, D.C., the Minnesota Historical Society, the State Historical Society of Wisconsin, the Ohio Historical Society, the Cincinnati Historical Society, the Georgia Department of Archives and History, the South Carolina Department of Archives and History, the Caroliniana Room at the University of South Carolina Library, the South Carolina Historical Society, and the State Historical Society of North Dakota.

Chronology

1824, 12 February, born at Mount Vernon, Ohio
1842-late 1840s, taught in rural schools around Crestline, Ohio
1849, married Mary Jane Mitchell, Mansfield, Ohio ca. 1850, Principal of a Grammar School in Columbus, Ohio
1853-1855, undergraduate student and Instructor, Literary Department, Ohio Wesleyan University, Delaware, Ohio
1855-1857, Principal, McNeely Normal School, Hopedale, Ohio
1858, Received Master of Arts degree, Ohio Wesleyan University
1859, published book, *The Science of Education and the Art of Teaching* (Cincinnati)
1860-1861, Founding Principal, Minnesota State Normal School, Winona
1861, enlisted in First Wisconsin Cavalry
1862-1865, Lieutenant, First Wisconsin Cavalry
1864-1865, Prisoner of War in South Carolina and Georgia; escaped and recaptured, 1864
1865, published partial account of Civil War experiences in A. O. Abbot, ed., *Prison Life in the South* (New York)
1865, appointed Superintendent of Education for the Freedmen's Bureau for Kentucky and Tennessee
1865 or 1866, divorced from Mary Jane Mitchell in Ohio
1866, August, married Anna Augusta Brewster in St. Paul, Minnesota
1866-1870, Principal, later President, of Fisk School / Fisk University, Nashville, Tennessee
1870-1871, Principal, Kenyon Grammar School, Kenyon College, Gambier, Ohio
1871-1881, co-proprietor (later Proprietor and Principal), Ohio Central Normal School, Worthington, Ohio
1878, published "Outlines of a Complete System of Pedagogical Science," 24 pages (Columbus)
1881-1882, Principal, Fayette Normal, Music, and Business College, Fayette (Fulton County), Ohio
1882-1885, Lived in Washington, D. C.
1887-1888, Superintendent of Schools, McIntosh County, Dakota Territory
1888-1889, Principal, Milnor State Normal School, Milnor (Sargent County), North Dakota
1890-1892, Superintendent of Public Instruction, State of North Dakota
1893-1907, in retirement, or semi-retirement, Minneapolis, Minnesota
1907-1910, lived in Seattle, Washington.
1910, 23 July, died in Seattle.

Introduction

John Ogden, 1824-1910, Ohio born and bred, one of the founders and the first leader of Fisk University, was one of the early participants in Southern Negro education. He narrowly missed inclusion in James McPherson's list of abolitionist men and women who carried on the decades-long anti-slavery struggle in a different form after the Civil War. When McPherson published his noted *Abolitionist Legacy* in 1975 he based the analysis on a study of 284 abolitionists prominent in the "legacy" period that ran from Reconstruction until the founding of the NAACP. McPherson included in the list the second and third presidents of Nashville's Fisk University, but not John Ogden who was the first.[1] Also on McPherson's list were several of Ogden's close colleagues in two Northern freedmen's aid societies—Levi Coffin of Cincinnati's Western Freedmen's Aid Commission—and Erastus M. Cravath, Edward Parmelee Smith, and Michael Strieby of New York's (and Cincinnati's) American Missionary Association; but in that context too McPherson left Ogden aside.

McPherson observed simply that he was unable to turn up enough information on Ogden to place him on the list.[2] No wonder this was so; John Ogden was a peripatetic professional educator and the information needed to construct a picture of him is scattered in eleven states and the District of Columbia. Ogden worked—or left documentary traces—in Ohio, Wisconsin, Minnesota, South Carolina, Tennessee, Georgia, New York, North Dakota, Oregon, Washington, D.C., Washington state, and Louisiana. He was a principal, president, or superintendent of at least nine different schools, county school systems, normal schools, or state departments of public instruction, and over several decades he conducted hundreds of teacher institutes in a half-dozen states.

---

[1] James M. McPherson, *The Abolitionist Legacy: From Reconstruction to the NAACP* (Princeton, 1975), 395 ff. Adam K. Spence was the second president of Fisk, Erastus M. Cravath the third.

[2] McPherson, personal communication, 1978. A number of the younger individuals on his list (born after 1850) got there through descent; they were second or third generation members of abolitionist families. Ogden's parents were no help there; we know nothing of their views on slavery.

Ogden deserves to be included in the "abolitionist legacy" because of his five-years' work with blacks in the South after the Civil War as first, an education superintendent in the Freedmen's Bureau, secondly an agent for the Western Freedmen's Aid Commission, and lastly as a founder and the first leader of Fisk University. The purpose here is to place these years in the context of his entire life and his teacher-training career in several sections of the United States. An important thing to understand about Ogden is that he was a professional educator with a penchant for reform rather than a reformer who worked in education. He had become familiar with the South during the Civil War when he spent three years there as an officer in a Wisconsin cavalry regiment and this acquaintanceship—even including eight months as a prisoner of war—left him willing to spend more time in Dixie to pursue his reforming emotions.

Bringing John Ogden to scholarly attention is a small part of the continuing effort of over thirty years' duration that has expanded knowledge of the less-famous abolitionists and their post-war work. McPherson, in his 1964 *Struggle for Equality: Abolitionists and the Negro in the Civil War and Reconstruction*,[3] began the enlargement, moving from a restricted emphasis on Garrison and well-known pre-war abolitionists to encompass a broader spectrum of participants. The work has continued, with later examples of studies of men linked to Ogden being a 1984 article on E.O. Tade in the *Tennessee Historical Quarterly* and the 1993 book-length biography of Edward Parmelee Smith.[4]

---

[3] Princeton, 1964.

[4] William H. Armstrong, *A Friend to God's Poor: Edward Parmelee Smith*, Athens, GA: University of Georgia Press, 1993. The earlier example on an obscure figure is C. Stuart McGehee, "E.O. Tade, Freedmen's Education, and the Failure of Reconstruction in Tennessee," *Tennessee Historical Quarterly* (Cited henceforth as THQ), 43 (Winter 1984): 376-389. Tade is so little-known that a respected scholar recently called him "Jade." See Dan T. Carter, *When the War Was Over: The Failure of Self-Reconstruction in the South, 1865-1867* (Baton Rouge: Louisiana State University Press, 1985), 151.

CHAPTER 1
Early Life in the Buckeye State and Midwestern Beginnings of a Normal-School Career

Typical of the modest social origins of most entrants into professional teaching, Ogden was born into a large farm family; his at Mount Vernon, Ohio. He was reared near Crestline, Ohio.[5] He began his teaching career in 1842 at age eighteen, first in a log-house common school at Crestline where he was paid $11 in cash per month and boarded around for the rest of his needs.[6] His youthful work and methods resembled those of many aspirants: he taught in semi-rural and small town schools during as much of each year as he could and slowly accumulated experience. Teaching through the 1840s, he married in 1849, a union whose failure later produced soul-searching misery for him.[7] In about 1850 he was named principal of a grammar school on Mound Street in Columbus, Ohio.

In 1853, almost thirty years old, Ogden entered Ohio Wesleyan University at Delaware, Ohio, near Columbus and Crestline, to pursue a bachelor's degree.[8] While an undergraduate at Wesleyan he taught in the

---

[5] William Ogden Wheeler, *The Ogden Family in America* (Philadelphia, 1907), 262; 379-380.

[6] Dorene Heacock Larimer, "Evaluation of John Ogden—Educator," B. A. thesis, Pacific College, Newberg, Oregon [now George Fox College], 1933, 83. Larimer was Ogden's grand-daughter-in-law and had access to family papers, files, and verbal traditions. Interview, Don Larimer, Portland, Oregon, 1985.

[7] Ogden wed Mary Jane Mitchell in Mansfield, Ohio, 5 July 1849. A daughter, Clara, was born in 1854. The Ogdens separated in about 1859, Mrs. Ogden apparently refusing to live with Ogden (See Appendix); they divorced in 1865. Wheeler, *Ogden Family*, 379-380; A. A. Taylor, "Fisk University, 1866-1951: A Constructive Influence in American Life," unpublished MS, Amistad Research Center, Tulane University, New Orleans (Cited henceforth as Amistad), 44-46; Ogden, Manuscript Journal of Verse, 1861-1865, in possession of Ogden descendants; copy in author's possession; pp. 24-26, 59-61, 120, 122-124, 129, 134, 136, and 139 (Cited henceforth as Ogden Journal); Ogden Military Pension Record, John Ogden, 1st Wisconsin Cavalry, Civil War, National Archives, Washington, DC (Cited henceforth as Ogden Pension Record, NA).

[8] Larimer, "Evaluation of Ogden," 12. Personal communication, John H. Reed, Ohio Wesleyan Archives, 1975.

"Literary" (preparatory) department for two years while he worked on his own degree. He did not graduate with his 1856 class, however, but left campus to earn money teaching full-time, an enlargement of the self-support that he had generated teaching part time.[9] In November 1855 he became "President and Principal" of the McNeely Normal School (including the usual preparatory department), at Hopedale, Ohio, not far from Wheeling, Virginia. Hopedale was a rustic little town off the rail lines where Ogden remained until October 1857, resigning because of fundraising discouragements. This was the first of his several start-up assignments, later to include Fisk.[10]

After leaving McNeely Ogden let no grass grow under his feet; he returned to Ohio Wesleyan and soon completed the requirements for the *Artium Magister* which he received in 1858.[11] Master's degrees were few, and the academic distinction, added to his leadership experience, positioned him for career advancement. After receiving the degree Ogden spent a year and a half conducting "teachers' institutes" and finalizing for publication a textbook, *The Science of Education and the Art of Teaching*, based in part upon his McNeely teaching experience. This fat book was reprinted at least eight times in two editions, though there is no indication that Ogden made any money from it.[12]

---

[9] Reed, Ohio Wesleyan Archives.

[10] See Illustration 1. R.H. Eckelberry, "The McNeely Normal School and Hopedale Normal College," *Ohio Archaeological and Historical Publications* 50 (1931): 86-136, esp. 86-115.

[11] Ogden graduated owing tuition; in an October 1865 letter, Ohio Wesleyan University President Frederick Merrick said that he could not get Ogden out of his university debt, and "as it is we lose about $200." American Missionary Association Archives (Cited henceforth as AMA), Amistad. Merrick was a friend; in December 1864 he sent Prisoner of War Ogden $25 at Camp Sorghum, Columbia, SC, with which he bought badly-needed shoes. John Ogden, unpub. MS, "Adventures and Escapes," 85-86, Record Group 31: Civil War Small Collections, Ogden File, Wisconsin Veterans Museum, Madison. The MS is pencil on dark brown paper, accompanied by a transcription to which all page references are made. (Cited henceforth as Ogden, "Adventures and Escapes," page, WVM.) Merrick and Ogden worked together until at least 1875. See "Fourth Annual Catalogue of the Instructors' Lecturers and Students of the Ohio Central Normal School, 1875-76, Worthington, Franklin Co., Ohio."

[12] Ogden, *The Science of Education and Art of Teaching* (Cincinnati: Moore, Wilstach, Keys & Co., 1859). 478 p.; 8th ed. by "Cincinnati Steam Press" dated 1868. Two-volume ed., *The Science of Education; or the Philosophy of Human Culture*, and *The Art of Teaching* (Cincinnati, New York: Van Antwerp, Bragg, & Co., 1879); on sales, see

Early Life

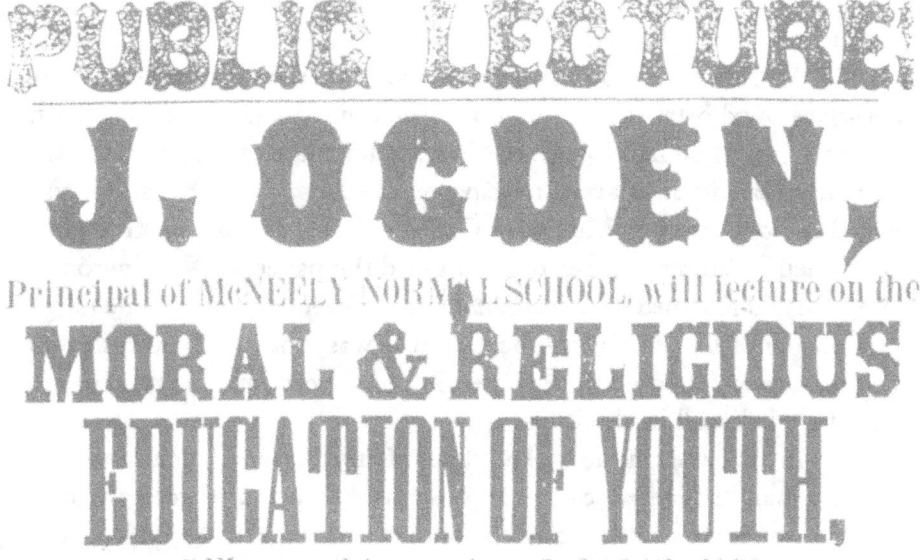

1. Flyer for John Ogden talk, McNeely Normal School, Hopedale, Ohio, 1856. From the Collection of the Ohio Historical Center, Columbus.

---

especially 18 November 1867 when they wrote, "Your book is selling regularly but slowly." AMA, Amistad.

The many teachers' institutes that Ogden led around this time were usually in the Midwest, though one seems to have been as far off as Pennsylvania. These institutes were five-to-seven-day-long teacher-training and educational-publicity gatherings (similar to the later Chautauquas) that aimed to improve teachers' skills and ignite citizen enthusiasm for public schools.

Also during these years Ogden continued to take seriously the anti-slavery exhortations of the more ardent members of the Methodist Church, just as he had for years. From at least age twenty-two Ogden regularly read an antislavery newspaper, the *Herald and Philanthropist*, edited and published by Methodist Gamaliel Bailey in Cincinnati. Ogden continued to subscribe after Bailey moved the paper to Washington in late 1846 and renamed it the *National Era*.[13] Given Ogden's later-evident passionate hostility to slavery, he probably was not merely anti-slavery before the war (opposed to the extension of slavery into the territories), but likely believed in abolition.[14]

In 1859 the educational publicist Henry Barnard, then serving as the top man in state education in Wisconsin, heard of Ogden through intermediaries, and invited him to conduct institutes in the Badger state in the fall of that year.[15] Barnard, perhaps the most famous man in nineteenth-century American education after Horace Mann, has always been overrated according to the evaluation of his most recent biographer, but Barnard helped John Ogden substantially at this time.[16] In 1859 Barnard was just beginning another of his short-tenure and not very

---

[13] Ogden's religious affiliation at this time is not totally certain. Apparently his family had him baptized as a Baptist, but his many years of work with Methodists led many people to consider him a member of that faith. In later years he was sometimes active as a Methodist but more commonly participated in the Episcopal Churches that his wife attended. See below the discussion of possible religious-affiliation reasons for his departure from Fisk University in 1870 and his religious activities in the 1880s in North Dakota.

[14] Stanley Harrold, *Gamaliel Bailey and Antislavery Union* (Kent, OH; Kent State University Press, 1986), 71, 82; Larimer, "Evaluation of Ogden," 177-178; 180-181; Ogden,. "Adventures and Escapes," 10, WVM.

[15] Ogden to Barnard, 25 August 1859, accepting. *Cf.* June-July 1859 rejections from others. Henry Barnard Papers, folders 122-123, Fales Library, Bobst Library, New York University.

[16] Edith Nye MacMullen, *In the Cause of True Education: Henry Barnard and Nineteenth-Century School Reform* (New Haven: Yale University Press, 1991). MacMullen converted Buckeye John Ogden into a Pennsylvanian, 226.

Early Life 7

successful jobs as Chancellor of the University of Wisconsin and agent for the Board of Regents of the Wisconsin Normal Schools. As part of the latter assignment, Barnard and his assistants organized fourteen Wisconsin teacher institutes in the fall of 1859. They summoned the experienced Ogden to serve as a lecturer at a number of these meetings. Moreover, Barnard, wherever he lived, usually served as an informal job agency and at this time provided such a service for Ogden, apparently recommending him to the board of the newly-founded Minnesota Normal School at Winona, just across the Mississippi River from Wisconsin.[17]

Ogden was eager to accept the position the board eventually offered him in then-frontier Minnesota for not only did he need a job but he later hinted that he had desired to go far away from his estranged wife. This Victorian man, seriously distressed by the dissolution of his marriage to Mary Jane Mitchell, poured out his heart in his poetry journal over the next several years in sometimes extravagant phrases such as

> Forsaken by the wife I wed
> I am undone, *I am undone*

that showed that in that Victorian era he required a long time to adjust to his situation and "get on with his life" as modern cliché might phrase it.[18]

The move to Winona thus reflected not only his need for a job and a desire to distance himself from his wife in Ohio (futile therapy in

---

[17] William H. Herrmann, *The Rise of the Public Normal School System in Wisconsin* (Madison, 1971), 92, 122-123. Ogden to Barnard, 19 September—31 December 1859, Barnard Papers, folders 124-128, Fales Library, New York University; Jonathan D. Ford, Board Secretary, Minnesota State Normal School, to Barnard, 14 October and 30 November 1859. Barnard Papers, folders 124-128, New York University; Jean Talbot, "The First State Normal School, 1860: Winona State College, 1960," in *Quarterly Bulletin of Winona State College, 1959-1960*, 1-3; "Historical Sketch and Notes," n.p., n.d., 32-34, cited in Larimer, "Evaluation of Ogden," 13-14.

[18] These lines are from a poem entitled, "Past Time," dated 27 July 1863 at Salem, Tennessee. See Appendix of selected Poems and Writings of John Ogden for other examples from Ogden Journal. The only information I have been able to glean about Ogden and his first wife come from the poetry which could easily be misinterpreted. At times it sounds as though he is talking about adultery, while at other times he seems to suggest that wagging, jealous tongues were the cause of the troubles. Unless entirely new information comes to light I doubt that even approximate certainty can be attained in understanding this domestic disagreement.

the near term as the 1863-1864 poems clearly show), but it also hinted at a life-long penchant—to which he several times yielded, even when his domestic situation was stable—to move to new places and take new jobs that were on the geographical and professional edge. In 1860 no doubt his rootlessness and desire for an appropriate leadership position had an effect, but Minnesota—whose population rose from 6,000 in 1850 to 172,000 the year Ogden started there—lured him with a promise of change and adventure that he succumbed to until surprisingly late in life.[19]

During Ogden's tenure as Principal of Minnesota's first state teachers college he gave several speeches that offer insight into his beliefs—those probably still ruling when he began serving as Fisk's leader in Nashville five years later. In his 1860 Winona inaugural address he said that "every child, white, red, or black, male or female, bond or free, rich or poor, high or low, domestic or foreign, has an inalienable right to an education." A normal-school leader who said that in 1860 would certainly be a candidate for educational work with blacks in the South after the war. In 1860 Ogden also spoke of the teacher professionalism that partly motivated him for the last sixty years of his life. He said that "teaching is just as distinctly, essentially, and emphatically a profession, to be learned by observation, study and practice, as any other."[20] Beginning teaching as he had in 1842, Ogden was in virtually the first cohort of the new, self-conscious education profession. He had entered just after the period when male school teachers were largely regarded as unqualified n'er-do-wells who taught because they could do nothing else.[21] Ogden and his generation believed in formal teacher-training instruction, and strove to make teaching a *profession*. He did this not only at Winona, but in all the other normal schools he administered for the rest of his life.

Given the Yankee Ogden was, and his powerful feelings about

---

[19] *Historical Statistics of the United States: Colonial Times to 1970* (Washington, 1975), Part 1, Series A 195-209, p. 30.

[20] Ogden, "Inaugural Discourse," in Edward Duffield Neill and John Ogden, *Addresses Delivered at the Opening of the State Normal School, Winona, Minnesota, with a report of the course of Instruction and Other Documents. Published by the Prudential Committee.* (Saint Paul, 1860), 15-35. See Appendix for full text. See also Burton J. Bledstein, *The Culture of Professionalism: The Middle Class and the Development of Higher Education in America* (New York, 1976). Ogden's status was much more modest than that of the eminent university presidents Bledstein studied.

[21] Larimer, "Evaluation of Ogden," 83.

Early Life

the wrongness of slavery, the secession of the Southern states upset him, though he believed that the Union armies would quickly suppress the revolt. The Union defeat at First Bull Run on 21 July 1861 shattered his composure. He expressed his feelings in poetry as he often did when overwrought. Before the battle he had written:

> Go, conquer tyrants, free the Slave!
> Baptize your freedom fresh in blood.
> Lift high the Banner, let it wave,
>   And fight for Country, home and God.
> And with returning battle shout,
> I wipe the stain of slavery out.

After the Northern defeat he wrote:

> They went, they fought, and round them fell
> The flower, the glory of the Land.
> And oh, I blush the truth to tell,
> They fled before the accursed band.
> In Israel's Camp an idol lay
> That troubled freedom's hosts that day.[22]

Ogden stayed on as chief at Winona until December of 1861 when he resigned to enter the army. In his resignation letter he said that his "dishonored country calls louder for my poor service just now than the school does," and "I feel ashamed to tarry longer."[23] Taken altogether, we can accept at face value his stated reasons for enlisting. He definitely shared the Union goal of victory over the Secessionists and in 1861 probably felt the lure of travel and the excitement of a change from routine. Though he continued for several more years to bemoan his fractured marriage, his enlistment was not a wish to court danger or death. Ogden oftentimes demonstrated the maudlin sentimentality of his era, but he never hinted at a death wish. While suffering emotionally, he saw Army service as a way to stay busy, do some good and forget—not as a way to get hurt. Thus at age thirty-seven, with his small and much-

---

[22] Poem "A Prophecy," Ogden Journal, pp. 3-4; see also Larimer, "Evaluation of Ogden," 169.

[23] Ogden to Prudential Committee, First State Normal School of Minnesota, 14 December 1861, quoted in Larimer, "Evaluation of Ogden," 3.

loved daughter and his estranged wife in Ohio (but leaving in Minnesota a promising new student female acquaintance whose existence he seems not to have been fully able to admit even to himself), Ogden located an army billet that offered potential.[24]

---

[24] At Winona Ogden met and perhaps even courted the much younger woman student, Anna Augusta Brewster (born Wisconsin, 1842, died Seattle, 1908) of St. Paul, whom he married in 1866.

CHAPTER 2
Civil War Interruptions: Lieutenant Ogden and the First Wisconsin Cavalry

Ogden enlisted in the First Regiment of Wisconsin Cavalry two weeks after Edward Daniels was promoted Colonel and named its commander. Although Ogden entered as a private, he probably expected something better to turn up and may well have seen Daniels as the likely vehicle. Daniels, described by McPherson as a "typical Yankee entrepreneur-reformer," had moved to Wisconsin from New England. After the war, he moved South, invested heavily—and lost heavily. Ogden might readily empathize with a man of that type and wish to serve in his regiment.[25] Furthermore, in September 1860 Daniels had become a Regent on the Wisconsin Normal School Board, had therefore an empathy for education and familiarity with it, and Ogden may even have known him in that connection.[26]

In Wisconsin, as in the South, some men sought the cavalry over the more numerous and mundane infantry. To enter the horseback elite with the hope of becoming an officer, it helped to have something in common with the regimental commander and the company commander. It also helped to bring along companions. When Ogden enlisted on 20 December 1861 in the First Wisconsin Cavalry's Company M he brought along nine young recruits, most from Winona or Red Wing, Minnesota, three his former students.[27]

The war kept Ogden close to colleagues in education. Colonel Daniels represented the Board level. Captain Thomas J. Conatty,

---

[25] McPherson, *Abolitionist Legacy* 76; Roster, Co. M, 1st Wisconsin Cavalry Regiment, Record Group 31: Civil War Small Collections, First Wisconsin Cavalry Regiment File, Wisconsin Veterans Museum, Madison. (Cited henceforth as Roster, 1st Wisc. Cav., WVM.)

[26] Silas Chapman, Board Secretary, to Daniels, 28 September 1860, Edward Daniels Papers, Archives-Manuscripts Division, State Historical Society of Wisconsin, Madison. (Cited henceforth as SHSW.)

[27] Roster, 1st Wisc. Cav., WVM. One student, Sgt. George T. Gray, later captured with Ogden, died in prison camp at Florence, SC, 15 September 1864. *Roster of Wisconsin Volunteers, War of the Rebellion, 1861-1865*, 2 vols. (Madison, 1886), I, 44; Ogden, "Adventures and Escapes," 28-29, WVM.

principal of Kenosha, Wisconsin, high school commanded Ogden's company (M) as it formed at Racine, Wisconsin. When Ogden was commissioned six months later as second lieutenant in the company, he replaced John A. Owen, a Milwaukee school teacher who moved up to first lieutenant.[28] Most of the others left the Army before the war was over, but Ogden stayed until the end—unwillingly as a prisoner in the South during most of the final year.

When the regiment's training was completed at Racine in early 1862 it moved to Missouri. Spending most of his time on relatively peaceful guard and patrol duty, Ogden on 19 October 1862 was placed in command of a detachment of twenty cavalrymen which accompanied three hundred infantrymen from the Missouri State Militia (under the command of a Missouri State Militia colonel), two hundred other infantrymen, and two pieces of artillery on a scout into southern Missouri and southeast Kansas in search of guerrilla bands.[29] No results are reported from this expedition, but Ogden the following year did get caught in one sanguinary fracas, perhaps one of the "dozen battles" that he later claimed to have participated in by 1864.[30]

By then promoted to First Lieutenant of Company E, Ogden's tangle came on 24 April 1863. His Company E commander, Captain S. V. Shipman, with forty men, was guarding a bridge over the Whitewater River, sixteen miles outside of Cape Girardeau. During the night, Ogden and twenty men galloped into the camp to tell Shipman that one of Marmadukes' Confederate columns with 3,000 men had surrounded the company and that they were going to have to cut their way out. During the charge, Capt. Shipman was hit in the thigh, knocked from his horse, and captured. Other troopers were wounded too, with Ogden allegedly "leaving his sabre driven to the hilt through the body of his last

---

[28] Wisconsin Adjutant General to Col. Daniels, Commanding First Wisc. Cav., Cape Girardeau, 3 July 1862, Daniels Papers, SHSW; Roster, 1st Wisc. Cav., WVM.

[29] "Compiled Records Showing Service of Military Units of Volunteer Union Organizations," National Archives Microfilm Publication M 594, Roll 197, 'M' Co, 1st Regt Wisc. Cav.

[30] Ogden, "Adventures and Escapes," 5, WVM. Military Record, John Ogden, Companies M & E, 1st Wisconsin Cavalry, Civil War, National Archives, Washington, DC. (Cited henceforth as Ogden Military Record, NA). Oscar H. LaGrange to Ogden, 10 October 1907, Ogden Papers, in author's possession. These papers, about 1.5 cubic feet, were given to the author by Ogden's descendants. Following publication of this biography he intends to offer them to the Amistad Research Center, Tulane University, New Orleans.

antagonist." Union sources admit that Co. E lost twenty-one killed, wounded, or captured, including four Privates killed. Ogden didn't talk about this incident much, and only once, twenty years later, recalling an entirely different episode, alluded to this Missouri skirmish, saying "My first impulse was to draw my sabre and run him through, as I had done with a better man on another occasion, though in a fair battle."[31]

In all wars of course, both sides win at least the skirmishes. Thus the report of Rebel commander George W. Carter told a different story: "The enemy's force consisted of Company G [E] (Captain Shipman), First Wisconsin Cavalry. They fought bravely; were 57 strong. Of this number 40 were destroyed, either killed, captured or wounded.... My loss was 4 wounded." Could Ogden have run a sabre through a trooper who ended up only wounded? The reader may decide even though years later Ogden still asserted that he had done it.[32]

With Shipman's removal from the scene, Ogden acted as company commander into the summer of 1863 as the First Wisconsin Cavalry moved to Tennessee. There he went off on detached service, either to recruit colored troops—which he did on different occasions in 1863 and 1864—or to serve on the Department of the Cumberland Examination Board for Signal Corps Officers which he was also detailed to do. Recruiting for the new Negro regiments, a move authorized in spring 1863, was probably a comfortable activity for Ogden. Since most of the 180,000 blacks who entered the Army were recruited (impressed in certain abusive cases) in the border states, Ogden probably spent his recruiting time in or near Tennessee. For the Signal Corps Examination Board he was a natural given his education and teaching experience. Practiced in giving exams, he could readily discern if the officer candidates applying for the Signal Corps had the relatively higher

---

[31] Ogden was promoted 1st Lt. in November 1862. Ogden Military Record, NA; William DeLoss Love, *Wisconsin in the War of the Rebellion: A History of all Regiments and Batteries* (Chicago, 1866, 562; E.B. Quiner, *The Military History of Wisconsin: A Record of the Civil and Military Patriotism of the State in the War for the Union* (Chicago, 1866), 886-887; *Roster of Wisconsin Volunteers, 1861-1865*, II, 1-49; unidentified clipping, *National Tribune* [ca. 1899], First Wisc. Cav. File, WVM; Ogden, "Adventures and Escapes, 3, WVM.

[32] Report of George W. Carter, 5 May 1863, *The War of the Rebellion: A Compilation of the Official Records of the Union and Confederate Armies* (69 vols. and index; Washington, 1880-1901; cited henceforth as OR), Series 1, Vol. 22, Pt. 1, 301. Ogden, "Adventures and Escapes," 3, WVM.

intellectual abilities needed for that service.[33]

For a man in his late thirties destined to live nearly a half-century more, Ogden ailed considerably in the war environment. Though he was big enough for effective cavalry service—six feet two or three inches, two hundred pounds (grey eyes incidentally)—and big enough for a horse to have some work to do when charging with him on his back, Ogden was no longer a youth, and for twenty years before entering the Army had performed non-physical classroom and administrative tasks.

His first medical problem came in Missouri when he smashed his dentures on hardtack and could neither give understandable orders to his men nor eat properly. After some delay he was allowed to go to St. Louis for four days in February 1863 to get his false teeth set into a new plate. Then when he was on duty (perhaps detached duty) in northern Alabama in late fall 1863, the surgeon of the 13th Wisconsin Infantry at Stevenson, Alabama, sent him home on medical leave to Crestline, Ohio, with "chronic diarrhoea" and related troubles. Ogden spent the winter, from about 10 November 1863 until about 23 February 1864, recuperating in or near Crestline before he reported back to his unit near Loudon and Madisonville, Tennessee (in eastern Tennessee between Chattanooga and Knoxville), during the first week of March 1864. Ogden later misleadingly—even dishonestly—termed this a "short furlough." At least the diarrhea, chronic inflammation of the bowels, and hemorrhoids did not kill him as they did so many others, and this man who entered his fifth decade of life on 12 February 1864 returned to duty with enough strength to survive another year of campaigning around Atlanta, lolling in prisoner-of-war camps, and creeping through the South Carolina countryside as a wintertime escapee. Ogden definitely did not lack the courage or the fortitude to press forward when many younger men dropped by the wayside.[34]

---

[33] Ogden Military Record, NA; War Dept. General Orders No. 106, 28 April 1863, OR, Series III, vol. 3, 172-174; No. 223, 17 July 1863, OR, Series III, vol. 3, 172-174 and vol. 4, 818-819; Major George L. Stearns, Commissioner for Organization of Colored Troops, to Stanton, 11 September 1863, OR, Series III, vol. 3, 785-787.

[34] Ogden never mentioned false teeth; the information is found only in his Military Record, NA. Ogden received many extensions from Army surgeons in Ohio in those months. Would a young enlisted man without his status and rank have been allowed to recuperate at home all winter? The First Wisconsin Cavalry did some fighting in December and January, 1863-1864, which Ogden missed. See John W. Rowell, *Yankee Cavalrymen: Through the Civil War with the Ninth Pennsylvania Cavalry* (Knoxville,

Ogden also spent some time in the Officer's Military Hospital in Chattanooga in September or October, 1863, after the Union defeat at Chickamauga (19-20 September). He nursed another officer who was dying, but whether as a fellow-patient helping the officer in the next bed, or aiding someone from his regiment is not clear.[35]

While Ogden's journal of poetry composed during the war is most interesting for its revelation of his attitudes toward marriage and the dissolution of his marriage, the time of the Union defeat at Chickamauga was one of the worst that Ogden saw during the entire war, and it brought out of him verse as extravagantly sentimental as any he ever penned. While all of his poetry was the product of its time, he was slightly more straightforward when he wrote about himself than when he engaged conventional topics such as death on the battlefield. His poem, "The Dying Soldier on the Battlefield of Chickamauga," attains in verse eight a peak of lurid sentimentality:

> Near my Heart you'll find her picture
> > Clasped in pearly links of gold,
> Take it, and entwine this message
> > With locks of tender fold.
> Dip them in the blood here flowing
> > And convey them to my dove.
> Tell her thus I seal forever
> > All our earthly vows of love.[36]

Although the First Wisconsin Cavalry participated in the Atlanta Campaign beginning in May 1864, Ogden was not there to see its end in September. He was captured by a rebel squad wearing Union Army uniforms on 5 June 1864, thirty miles from Marietta at Burnt Hickory, Georgia, "while," as he wrote, "looking after fugitive slaves that were anxious to join our ranks."[37] Except for two weeks on the lam that

---

1971), 157-167; Ogden Journal, 50, 51, 122, and 145.

[35] Ogden Military Record, NA; Poem, "The Dying Soldier on the Battlefield of Chickamauga, Sept. 19th 1863," dated 28 October 1863 in the Hospital, Chattanooga, Tennessee, in Ogden Journal, pp. 108-111. See also Larimer, "Evaluation of Ogden, 174-176.

[36] Ogden Journal, 108-111.

[37] "Adventures and Escapes," 3-15, WVM. Quotation p. 3. He called it Burnt Hickory Springs; on muster rolls it was called Dallas, Georgia.

December, he remained until February 1865 in Confederate prisons in Macon and Savannah, Georgia; and Charleston and Columbia, South Carolina after which time he was moved northward and paroled.[38] The last hospitalization he mentioned was for three weeks at "Rebel Hospital," Columbia, South Carolina, October 1864.[39]

From "Camp Sorghum," Columbia, South Carolina, Ogden and a companion, Lt. George W. Kirkpatrick of the Fifteenth Iowa Infantry, escaped and roamed for seventeen days in late November and early December 1864, reaching the Savannah River outside Augusta, Georgia, before being recaptured. Ogden described the Iowa officer as a "steady, sensible young man who was willing to risk it."[40]

Escape from Camp Sorghum was easy, staying out difficult.[41] So many hundreds of Union officers walked away from Camp Sorghum that several days before Ogden and Kirkpatrick began *their* trek toward the Edgefield, South Carolina, jail, the newspaper there complained in these terms:

> Errant Yankees
> They seem to be everywhere; they actually cover the land like the locusts in Egypt. Ten have been lodged in our jail since Friday night last—all fugitives from Columbia.... Were not our people so commendably vigilant in arresting these vagrants, great evil might be the result of their wanderings .... This matter—the straggling of Yankee prisoners all over the country—is becoming very serious. Look to it in Columbia.[42]

---

[38] From Macon to Wilmington, except for the escape time, he and hundreds of Union officers moved together from camp to camp. See A.O. Abbott, ed., *Prison Life in the South: At Richmond, Macon, Savannah, Charleston, Columbia, Charlotte, Raleigh, Goldsborough, and Andersonville During the Years 1864 and 1865* (New York, 1865), 58-191. For Ogden's camp teaching, July 4th episode, and poems, see 68, 78, 81-83, 121-123. Ogden authored Chap. 16, "Escaped and Recaptured," 260-295. Officers fared better than enlisted men, supplementing issue rations with purchases, even executing bills of exchange payable in the North. See 160-162.

[39] Ogden Pension Record, NA. See also Abbott, ed., *Prison Life in the South*, 123.

[40] Ogden, "Adventures and Escapes," 29, WVM; Abbott, ed., *Prison Life in the South*, 346; *Roster and Records of Iowa Soldiers in the War of the Rebellion* (Des Moines, 1908), II, 972.

[41] William Hesseltine, *Civil War Prisons: A Study in War Psychology* (New York, 1965; first pub. 1930), 166; Ogden, "Adventures and Escapes," 29, WVM.

[42] *Edgefield Advertiser*, Edgefield, SC, 30 November 1864.

Civil War Interruptions 17

The Pursuit of Knowledge under Difficulties.

2. "The Pursuit of Knowledge under Difficulties," artist's depiction of Lt. John Ogden and Lt. George W. Kirkpatrick attempting to read a road sign at night in South Carolina during escape attempt, December 1864. From A.O. Abbott, ed., *Prison Life in the South: At Richmond, Macon, Savannah, Charleston, Columbia, Charlotte, Raleigh, Goldsborough, and Andersonville During the Years 1864 and 1865* (New York, 1865). p. [271]. Illustrates Ogden's account of the incident in Chap. 16, "Escaped and Recaptured." pp. 260-295.

A few days after this commentary several civilians captured Ogden and Kirkpatrick and lodged them in the same building.

During the seventeen days they were loose, though they had many customary escape experiences, they also had some unusual encounters. Considering Ogden's dubious health in the preceding twenty-four months, his age, the six months' P.O.W. regimen preceding the escape, and the difficulty of finding food and water while stumbling through South Carolina at night, he held up reasonably well. Kirkpatrick was younger, but that was offset in part because he had been many more months a P.O.W. During the parts of the seventeen days when they were in the care of slaves they ate better than at any time since they had entered the South, but when on the move thirst was often a greater problem than hunger.

3. "Recaptured," artist's depiction of Ogden and Kirkpatrick treed by dogs and captured, near Edgefield, S.C., from Abbott, ed., *Prison Life*, p. 289.

Immediately at the end of the war Ogden published an account of his imprisonment and escape and in about 1885-1887 elaborated the piece into a longer manuscript, made revealing changes, and added useful detail about his education, Masonic affiliation, abolitionist periodicals subscribed to, texts taught from—especially works proving God's existence—and other matters.[43] Both versions contained generic matter; most ex-prisoners recounted similar hardships. The major study of Civil War incarceration suggests that Ogden's account, one of the first published, told a story that soon became familiar.[44]

---

[43] Ogden, "Escaped and Recaptured," in Abbott, ed., *Prison Life in the South*, 260-295. Abbott was a Methodist minister and wrote familiarly on that subject to Ogden. Abbott to Ogden, 13 November 1865, AMA, Amistad. Ogden, "Adventures and Escapes," 7, 10, 11, 13, 19, 26-27, 77, 79, WVM.

[44] Hesseltine, *Civil War Prisons*. See also Alonso Cooper, *In and Out of Rebel Prisons* (Oswego, NY, 1888) and Willard W. Glazier, *The Capture, The Prison Pen, and the Escape* (New York, 1868), which reproduced an Ogden poem (166-168).

The charge of telling nothing unusual was true of Ogden when he wrote of the thievishness of his military captors at Burnt Hickory, ill-treatment and bad food in camp, and the receipt of assistance from slaves after he escaped; but he also described surprising things. For instance, he and Kirkpatrick spent part of their escape time hiding in stables near the slave cabins on the South Carolina plantation of Barney Dunbar, brother-in-law of the late Confederate Lieutenant-Colonel Thomas Gresham Lamar, the hero of Secessionsville.[45] Among Dunbar's slaves were several young Africans who had been part of the last cargo of slaves imported into the United States, a wild scheme carried out in 1858 by Charles Augustus Lafayette Lamar (later Confederate Colonel) with his slave ship, the *Wanderer*.[46]

Charles A. L. Lamar had been famous—or infamous—in the period just before the War as a militant slave-owner who swore he would reopen the slave trade in violation of the Constitution and who actually organized one voyage in support of his beliefs. In this much-publicized case, Lamar, heading a syndicate, had purchased the yacht *Wanderer* at the New York Yacht Club, outfitted it in New York harbor for slaving, and gone to Africa almost openly. The ship returned to St. Andrew Sound near Brunswick, Georgia, with 407 young Africans still alive of the some 487 who had embarked. Of these survivors, the first 170 were transshipped up the Savannah River and dispersed in November and December 1858 to different plantations on the South Carolina side of the river, just below Augusta, Georgia, near Beech Grove and Horse Creek, where Dunbar's plantation was located. When Ogden was hiding there with Kirkpatrick in December 1864 he recalled the story of the *Wanderer* and connected some of the slaves he met with that famous series of events.[47]

---

[45] Thomas Gresham Lamar (1826-1862). Died in Charleston, SC, 17 October 1862 from wounds received at Battle of Secessionsville. His second wife, Sarah Adams Dunbar, was Barney Dunbar's sister.

[46] Charles A.L. Lamar, 1824-1865. See entry for Gazaway Bugg Lamar (his father), in *Dictionary of American Biography*. Charles Lamar was a fanatic in more than one respect; he was killed 16 April 1865, when he knew the War was over and lost, in what was in effect a suicide attack on the 7th New York at Columbus, Georgia.

[47] Tom H. Wells, *Slave Ship Wanderer* (Athens, GA: University of Georgia Press, 1967), 28-29; see also Gene Gleason, "The Wanderer: Racing Yacht to Slave Ship," *Southern Exposure*, March/April 1984: 59-62; Ogden, "Adventures and Escapes," 53-58, WVM. Written more than twenty-five years after the events, Ogden got some details wrong.

He and Kirkpatrick had come into Dunbar's vicinity after steadily moving southward from their prison camp near Columbia, South Carolina. Traveling at night for a week, they had gone sixty miles and fetched up at the Savannah River, the boundary between South Carolina and Georgia.[48] They were unable to cross the river into Georgia because the local landowners, knowing that many Yankee ex-prisoners were loose and trying to get over the river to reach Sherman on his way to Savannah, removed or guarded all small craft and extensively patrolled the banks of the river and nearby roads.

At sunrise on Saturday, 3 December 1864, the two escapees, having luckily missed patrols and checkpoints, were hiding in the fog in heavy brush near the river road. They heard people coming down the road and could tell from the voices that they were negroes. "They seemed jolly and were singing and talking," Ogden wrote. He went up on the road to ask them to bring food, as he had done with blacks several times that week. A couple of the slaves ran off in fear, but some stayed. After learning who he was—not the first Federal escapee they had seen—the leader said that he would take them back up the road to the slave cabins of the Barney Dunbar plantation where "Granny" would feed them, and where they could hide. At that moment, with Sherman approaching Augusta, a short distance away on the other side of the river, Barney Dunbar was in the swamp hiding and protecting his horses and mules, thus leaving the slave cabin area of his plantation a relatively safe haven.[49]

The young men led Ogden and Kirkpatrick to the cabins where "Granny" was in command; she made the decisions and gave the orders. For thirty-six hours she secreted them in a stable not far from the cabins until Dunbar's unexpected return forced a hasty evacuation at 11:00 p.m. on Sunday night.

While Ogden and Kirkpatrick had been resting in the stable, a number of slaves had come to look at them—as objects of curiosity. In describing this in 1865 Ogden was brief and complimentary, saying

---

Personal communications, Barney Dunbar Lamar, III, 1977, and Charles Black Hammond (both Augusta, GA), 1977-1978. See also Warren S. Howard, *American Slavers and the Federal Law, 1837-1862* (Berkeley: University of California Press, 1963), 145-146; "A Slave-Trader's Letter-Book," citing letter of 18 December 1858 from Charles A.L. Lamar, *North American Review*, 143 (November 1886): 456.

[48] Illustration 2.

[49] Ogden, "Adventures and Escapes," 52, WVM.

simply, "some of the younger boys [from the *Wanderer*] are still living. They are rare specimens indeed. Their language is scarcely intelligible, though one or two with whom I conversed are very bright and intelligent." His 1885 rendition was much fuller:

> Some of the younger boys [from the *Wanderer*] were still living and paid their visits to us in the stable. The two that ran when we first hailed them on the road were natives [Africans]. They were all rare specimens and some of them showed me their arms where they were branded or marked with hot iron. They told me also that it was the custom to knock a tooth out with a hammer and iron punch. I believe some of those had been treated in that way. Their language was scarcely intelligible, so much of their native tongue clung to them. For instance, in addressing me, one of them spoke as follows. 'De-a wi-ta man-a he-a steal-a we-a from-a de-a coast-a Africa-a.' They also described the process of gathering ivory, or the elephant tusks, in the same strange combination of tongues. All these specimens were a shiny black and could be distinguished readily from the American born.[50]

Ogden was apparently of different minds when he wrote the two versions, and of course no editor worked on the 1885 version, while the first may have been edited for publication. The emphases differ: immediately after the war he described the Africans he saw as having suffered, but noted that they were bright and intelligent. Twenty years later he more strongly emphasized their sufferings, observing not only that many died on the *Wanderer* but specifying that they died "the horrible death of suffocation in the hold of the ship, and were thrown over board." Yet, in 1885 he went on to emphasize their differentness—their Africanness, their missing teeth, their unusual speech, and he no longer described them as "bright and intelligent." Was the change in tone attributable to Ogden's five years of post-war experience in the South?[51]

In all likelihood Ogden and Kirkpatrick did meet young slaves

---

[50] Ogden, "Escaped and Recaptured," *Prison Life in the South*, 282; "Adventures and Escapes," 57-58, WVM.

[51] Ogden, "Escaped and Recaptured," *Prison Life in the South*, 282; "Adventures and Escapes," 57, WVM.

who had come on the *Wanderer*. African-born slaves were not unknown in the South after the Civil War, though most were aged.⁵²

While Barney Dunbar did not quite catch Ogden and Kirkpatrick in his stables, the Hamburg, South Carolina, newspaper the slaves brought the two Union officers soon convinced them that there was no use staying longer. They could not get over the river, and even if they did, Sherman had already passed Augusta, heading southeast. After four days in the care of Dunbar's slaves, with their clothes somewhat repaired, and well supplied with food, Ogden and his younger companion set their course northward, for Tennessee. Within two days, however, the December weather worsened with cold and rain, the two got careless, and having proceeded not more than thirty-five miles, blundered right up to a mounted picket; not long afterward several civilians with dogs pursued them, the dogs forced them up a tree, and they were soon captured. Before sending them off to the Edgefield Jail their captor, a Mr. Brunson, took them to a nearby plantation where the lady of the house gave them the most elegant meal in the most genteel circumstances they encountered in the South—a sort of brunch, with "meat pie, plenty of warm biscuit and butter," served on a "white table cloth, clean white plate, cup, and saucer, and all the refinements of home."⁵³

They walked the eight miles to Edgefield in a driving rain and when they arrived at the jail Ogden revealed to the jailor that he was a Mason, a member of Arcana Lodge #272 of Crestline. The jailor admitted that he was a Mason too and Ogden asked his assistance. In response, the turnkey gave him and Kirkpatrick the important privilege—since they were soaked and it was December—of drying off by a fire before being locked up in an unheated cell. The next day Ogden dispatched a note to a local lady whose name the jailor suggested, Mrs. William W. (Annetta Cole) Goodman, a New York-born clergyman's daughter, married to a Massachusetts-born butcher and Mason, living in Edgefield with their seven children. She had food delivered to Ogden and Kirkpatrick, and persuaded a local couple, Mr. and Mrs. David Brooks, a well-to-do and cultivated Connecticut-born couple in their sixties, to bring food also.

---

⁵² John W. De Forest, *A Union Officer in the Reconstruction* (New Haven, 1948), 55, for an example. It has been estimated that 40,000 Africans were brought into the U.S. between 1808 and 1858.

⁵³ Illustration 3. Ogden, "Adventures and Escapes," 75, WVM; "Escaped and Recaptured," *Prison Life in the South*, 291.

Examples of Yankee sympathizers assisting escapees in the South were not uncommon, but more often occurred in big cities or in mountainous areas where Union sympathy was strong.[54]

One of Ogden's major themes in the 1885 account of his escape was the assistance he received from slaves. In 1870 he cited personal gratitude to slaves as the reason he had taken up educational work among Negroes in the South after the war, but given the interest he had maintained in abolition and in education for years before the war, and given the recruiting he had done for black regiments during the war, it may be doubted that his motivations derived solely from the excellent treatment slaves gave him and Kirkpatrick while they were fugitives.[55]

From Edgefield Ogden and Kirkpatrick were returned by a series of conveyances to the prison camp at Columbia, South Carolina. They were there only a few weeks, however, as the end of the War was clearly coming into view, and the Confederate government was glad to ship its wards back north so long as they were under parole not to fight. After parole rumors had circulated in the camp for several weeks, all the Columbia prisoners were shipped to Charlotte, North Carolina, then haltingly across that state to Wilmington where they were paroled 1 March 1865, handed over the Union forces, and sent by boat to Annapolis. Ogden spent some of the last days or weeks of the war in the nearby Maryland Parole Camp. He received two days leave to visit Washington, was almost home in Columbus, Ohio on 15 April, and was mustered out of the Army there effective 15 May 1865.[56]

---

[54] Ogden, "Escaped and Recaptured," *Prison Life in the South*, 292-293; "Adventures and Escapes," 77-81, WVM; Carlee T. McClendon, *Edgefield Marriage Records: Edgefield, SC* (Columbia, SC: 1970), 59, 62; Manuscript Population Schedule, Edgefield County, South Carolina, Eighth Census of the United States, 1860, Edgefield, SC, 218-219; John H. Moore, *Research Materials in South Carolina* (Columbia, SC, 1967), 7.

[55] Ogden, "A Peculiar Call to Teach," *American Missionary* 14 (December 1870): 283, cited in Robert C. Morris, *Reading, 'Riting, and Reconstruction: The Education of Freedmen in the South, 1861-1870* (Chicago, 1981), 77-78, where Morris discusses teacher motivation. He misidentified Ogden as a Methodist Minister, 38. See also Ogden, "Adventures and Escapes," 52-64, WVM.

[56] Ogden, "Adventures and Escapes," 86, WVM; *Roster of Wisconsin Volunteers, 1861-1865*, II, 1-49; Ogden Military Record, NA; Ogden Journal, p. 58.

CHAPTER 3
Right Back South: Freedmen's Bureau Educator in Tennessee and Kentucky

Even before Ogden was mustered out in mid-May 1865 he had begun searching for a way to go back South and work in Freedmen's education. While looking, he stayed in the North, visiting his family, including his twelve-year-old daughter, and also tarrying in St. Paul, Minnesota, near his former Winona student, Anna Augusta (Gussie) Brewster, whom he married the following year.[57]

In the summer after the War's end confusion continued and interested Yankees debated what means they might use to assist the Freedmen. What help would be appropriate? What organizations would deliver it? During the war considerable general relief for freedmen, educational work with freedmen, and labor management of freedmen had been performed in Union-controlled areas, but the scale was small compared to the far-ranging responsibilities that fell to the Yankees across the South as the Confederacy was occupied section-by-section and finally disappeared in April 1865.[58]

In Tennessee, as elsewhere, in those years many details concerning the effective delivery of aid to Freedmen had to be sorted out—sometimes in abrasive conflict between and within the white, Northern, freedmen's-aid societies. Continual rearrangement and modification went on until the final defeat and termination of Reconstruction in 1877 virtually ended—or at any rate put into deep slumber—that particularly noteworthy characteristic of intellectual life in mid-nineteenth-century America—the concern of well-meaning Northerners for Negroes in the South.[59]

Education was the principal response the freedmen's aid societies

---

[57] H.S. Dewey (Toledo) to Ogden (Columbus), 14 July 1865; Charles M. Allen (Madison) to Ogden, 30 July 1865, both AMA, Amistad. Ogden and his first wife divorced in 1865 in Mansfield, Ohio, apparently only after he decided to marry Anna Augusta Brewster. Ogden Pension Record, NA. See also Freedmen's Bureau correspondence cited below.

[58] See Eric Foner, *Reconstruction: The Unfinished Revolution, 1863-1877* (New York, 1988), 77-123.

[59] Reconstruction, strictly defined, was short in Tennessee, ending in July 1866 when statehood was regained. More severe reaction came later, in 1869.

made to the nearly innumerable needs of the freedmen although basic relief did continue for some time. Virtually everyone, however, soon abandoned economic development as a potential course of action.[60] Although they may have desired to see the Freedmen thrive economically, the education-only attitude prevailed among the Yankee men and women who started Fisk and similar schools because they believed it worked in the North. They gave insufficient consideration to the different traditions in the two societies and to the fact that capitalism was maturing and rapidly bringing proletarianization, creating different conditions than those they had known in the North before the War. The "free labor" notions that the aid-society people held after the war were obsolete.[61]

In 1865 and in the years that followed the Northern education-aid organizations fought with each other over philosophy, religion, and money—especially the money that the relatively well-financed Freedmen's Bureau directed into their coffers until 1874. The aid organizations also vied for funds coming from churches and charitable donors in the North and in Great Britain.[62]

The cast of characters in the Northern aid societies who were involved in Southern Negro education was large, confusing, and constantly changing. The line-up of organizations was hardly less confusing than the personnel. Focusing on John Ogden, Fisk School and Fisk University, one encounters with frequency only the American Missionary Association (AMA) whose main headquarters was in New York, and the Western Freedmen's Aid Commission (WFAC), based in Cincinnati. These were the two non-governmental organizations that founded Fisk School. By one measure—the number of teachers supported in the field—the New York organization was about four times the size of the Cincinnati one.[63]

---

[60] McGehee described Tade, a minister and educational administrator in Chattanooga from 1865 until 1875, as exceptional in his grasp of the importance of economic development, but nevertheless wrote that "religion and education" were his principal efforts. "E.O. Tade," THQ 43: 378-379; 381.

[61] For a criticism of education only, see Ronald E. Butchart, *Northern Schools, Southern Blacks, and Reconstruction: Freedmen's Education, 1862-1875* (Westport, CT, 1980), 9-10. See McGehee, "Tade," THQ, 376, for a different attitude.

[62] Butchart, *Northern Schools, Southern Blacks*, best describes the fights, 77-95.

[63] For lists see Richard B. Drake, "American Missionary Association and the Southern

It was to the smaller one in his home state, however, that Ogden wrote on 3 May 1865 as he began his search for a Southern educational position. A few days later the Corresponding Secretary of the Western Freedmen's' Aid Commission, J.M. Walden, directed an answer to "Rev. John Ogden" in Columbus saying that if terms of employment could be agreed upon the Western Freedmen's Aid Commission would employ him, "as much in the capacity of an Agent as teacher, to look after all the interests of the work at all the points you would be required to visit."

4. Fisk School (later University), opened 1866 in former Army Hospital buildings in central Nashville. Courtesy of Fisk University Library's Special Collections.

Tennessee was not yet specified. Walden added that Ogden was known to the Western Freedmen's Aid Commission board—of which the leading member was Levi Coffin, its "General Agent" who, with friends, had founded it in 1863.[64]

Negro, 1861-1888," (Ph.D. diss., Emory Univ., 1957), Table II, 277, 13-14; Paul David Phillips, "A History of the Freedmen's Bureau in Tennessee," (Ph.D. diss., Vanderbilt University, 1964), 71-72; and Butchart, *Northern Schools, Southern Blacks*, Tables 1-3, pp. 5, 7, 11.

[64] J. M. Walden to Ogden, 11 May 1865, AMA, Amistad. Coffin, a well-known Quaker underground railroader fictionalized in *Uncle Tom's Cabin*, sided with evangelicals in

The Western Freedmen's Aid Commission took Ogden on its staff and sent him South as their agent. Ogden's first efforts were directed to Chattanooga and Georgia. On 17 July a Cincinnati book concern directed textbooks to him at the East Tennessee city.[65] The Western Freedmen's Aid Commission also supported his work in Macon, Georgia (his prison camp home of the preceding year), where he organized five schools with twelve colored teachers for 725 scholars and established a "teacher's home." In late July, using colored teachers, he started schools for 180 black children in Atlanta.[66]

It was via the Western Freedmen's Aid Commission that Ogden first came into contact with General Clinton B. Fisk, soon to be Assistant Commissioner of the Freedmen's Bureau for Tennessee, Kentucky, and northern Alabama. On 5 July 1865, after Fisk arrived in Nashville, Ogden sent him from Ohio a "list of schools, teachers, and pupils [that are] under [the] auspices of the W[estern] F[reedmen's] Aid Com[mission]."[67] Three weeks later the WFAC guaranteed Ogden's salary in the Freedmen's Bureau "should Genl Fisk think him to be the right man as Supt. of Schools" and when Fisk told them he would make the

---

1863 when the WFAC was founded, but years later wrote to Ogden that "Cravath is so full of C[ongregational]ism that he needs careful watching lest he should try to run this Machine on Congregational wheels and finally make a sectarian Machine of it." Coffin to Ogden, 19 February 1869, cited in Taylor, "Fisk University," unpub MS, 64, Amistad. Coffin, in his 1878 *Reminiscences* was not forthcoming about WFAC internal politics. See Drake, "American Missionary Association," 13-14, and Butchart, *Northern Schools, Southern Blacks*, 83.

[65] Sargent, Wilson & Hinkle to Ogden, c/o Col. T. J. Morgan, Commanding Colored Brigade, Chattanooga, 17 July 1865, AMA, Amistad.

[66] William P. Russell (Murfreesboro) to Michael E. Strieby, Corresponding Secretary, AMA, 28 August 1865; Ogden to Walden, 26 August 1865, both AMA, Amistad. Cincinnati was key; while Ogden never lived there, the city had his publisher, book dealers, and WFAC. Ogden directed books and supplies to Macon and Atlanta as late as March 1866 although an October 1865 letter said that he recommended closure of the schools in those cities. (Cravath to Strieby, 11 Nov. 1865, AMA, Amistad.) Ogden, Superintendent Education Department to Tennessee Assistant Commissioner, Bureau of Refugees, Freedmen, and Abandoned Lands, Record Group 105, 20 March 1866, p. 286, #23, NA (hereafter BRFAL, RG 105, NA). Available as NA Microfilm Publication M999, 34 Rolls, (hereafter M999, BRFAL, Roll number, and page reference). See also E. P. Smith's District Secretary report on Tennessee and Georgia dated 19 December 1865, in *American Missionary* 10:2 (February 1866): 33.

[67] Summary in Tennessee Asst. Commissioner, Letters Received, "O"s, 1865, 311, BRFAL, RG 105, NA. (M999, BRFAL, Roll 5, p. 311)

appointment they sent Ogden to Nashville to work for the General but also to continue as the Western Freedmen's Aid Commission agent.[68]

General Fisk was impatient then—and in both summers he served in Tennessee—to get schools throughout Tennessee and Kentucky into operation. On August 1 in his General's voice he told the WFAC's Walden in Cincinnati that Ogden "cannot be too expeditious in reporting for duty. I want the schools to commence on the first Monday in September." Ogden was off in central Ohio and Rev. Walden reflected the military influence, replying that he had "telegraphed to Lieut. Ogden at Columbus" to alert him. Walden had transferred Ogden from the church but only to put him back into the Army. Later he moved him to professor status.[69]

Fisk served as Freedmen's Bureau Assistant Commissioner for Tennessee and Kentucky from 26 June 1865 until 1 September 1866.[70] Under him in the first autumn Ogden supervised in Tennessee thirty-one schools with 111 teachers serving 7,251 students, and about half that many in Kentucky.[71]

Thus, in August 1865, Ogden arrived in Nashville and entered upon a year-long period as "Superintendent, Education and Field Service, Educational Department, Bureau [of] Refugees, Freedmen, and Abandoned Lands, Office [of] Assistant Commissioner" for Tennessee and Kentucky. He worked for an Army Bureau, reported to a General, but was paid by Ohio civilians.[72] Why? Because General Fisk had no other

---

[68] J.M. Walden, Corresponding Secretary, WFAC, to Fisk, Tennessee Asst. Commissioner, Letters Received, BRFAL, RG 105, NA, (M999, BRFAL, Roll 5, p. 449); Fisk to Walden, Letterbook p. 162, same, (M999, BRFAL, Roll 1, p. 70).

[69] Fisk to Walden, 1 Aug. 1865, Press Book of Letters Sent, 162, BRFAL, RG 105, NA (M999, BRFAL, Roll 1, 162); Walden to Fisk, 9 August 1865, Letters Received, 451, BRFAL, RG 105, NA (M999, BRFAL, Roll 5, 451.)

[70] Fisk's realm at first included Tennessee, Kentucky, and North Alabama. The latter was removed 6 October 1865, Kentucky a little later. In 1866 Ogden still asked for reports from Alabama; Phillips, "Freedmen's Bureau in Tennessee," 49, n. 12; Ogden to I.S. Arnold, Supt. Freedmen's Schools, Huntsville, Alabama, 15 January 1866, AMA, Amistad. J.B.T. Marsh, *The Story of the Jubilee Singers* (Boston, 1880), 9. Lucius S. Merriam, *Higher Education in Tennessee* (Washington, 1893), 261-262. Phillips, "Freedmen's Bureau in Tennessee," 46-50. Alphonso A. Hopkins, *The Life of Clinton Bowen Fisk* (New York: Negro Universities Press, 1969; first pub. 1888), 93-94.

[71] Letter H9147A, 28 June 1866, AMA. Amistad.

[72] Title on Ogden letterhead, 26 August 1865, AMA, Amistad. Joe Richardson, "Fisk

source of personnel money. Congress appropriated no funds for Freedmen's Bureau superintendents until 1866, assuming that Army people would do the job. Although the Western Freedmen's Aid Commission at first paid all of Ogden's salary, within months the American Missionary Association agreed to cover half of it.[73] However, the aid organizations received substantial financial assistance from the Freedmen's Bureau. Thus federal money was probably the ultimate source of much of Ogden's salary.

Ogden's hierarchical relationships were obviously tangled since the AMA supported Fisk School from its earliest organization in 1865, wielded most of the power on the Board that hired him as first Superintendent of the school, and eventually absorbed the Western Freedmen's Aid Commission. Yet, until Ogden left the Freedmen's Bureau in mid-1866, until the Fisk Board of Trustees decided its goals for the school in 1867, and until the AMA and WFAC merged in March 1870, the organizations operated cooperatively in Nashville under *ad hoc* arrangements. Thus in 1865-1866 Ogden reported to General Fisk in one capacity, to the Fisk School Board of Trustees in another, served as the WFAC's agent in Tennessee, and received half his own salary from the WFAC; he worked for three organizations at once—a distinctly untidy arrangement.[74]

University: The First Critical Years," THQ, 29:1 (1970): 25, cites April and June 1865 letters to Ogden in the Fiskiana Collection, Fisk University Library, as evidence of Ogden's appointment. One predates General Fisk's 18 May 1865 appointment and both precede his 26 June 1865 arrival in Nashville. I have been unable to use the Fiskiana Collection. Richardson made Ogden a veteran of the *Second* Wisconsin Cavalry. Richardson also wrote a good general history of Fisk University, but it offers little for this study since he established Ogden at Fisk and got him out of Tennessee, all in the first twenty pages. *A History of Fisk University, 1865-1946* (University, AL: University of Alabama Press, 1980), 2-20.

[73] Morris, *Reading, 'Riting, and Reconstruction*, 49, n 160. WFAC linked Ogden's continuing Freedmen's Bureau work to receipt of half his salary from the AMA, and they suggested that if he had too little time to work for the BRFAL, the AMA might not continue to pay half. The WFAC asked, therefore, if Ogden was looking to the WFAC for only half his pay, or if he expected all of it from them. R.S. Rust, Corresponding Secretary, WFAC, to Ogden, 29 January 1866, AMA, Amistad. Rust was a Methodist divine.

[74] Merriam, *Higher Ed. in Tennessee*, 261-62. Rust to Ogden, 29 January and 3 February 1866, AMA, Amistad. Augustus F. Beard, *A Crusade of Brotherhood* (New York, 1972; first pub. 1909), 151. Double jobholding and moves back and forth between the aid

Two months after starting as Superintendent of Schools for Tennessee, Kentucky, and northern Alabama, Ogden began participating in the search for a place in Nashville to house a forthcoming "Fisk School" and a few months later he became its first "Superintendent" (which later became "Principal" and finally "President").[75] His salary for that work seems not to have been separate from, or in addition to, the pay he got for the Freedmen's Bureau work; and he continued as agent for the Western Freedmen's Aid Commission.

Why the confusion among the three organizations? Doing work that had never been done before in a place that had never seen such an undertaking presented a situation that required several years to straighten out. As of spring 1866 the Fisk School letterhead showed the structure:[76]

AMA	WFAC
Rev. E.P. Smith, Secty for Middlewest, Cincinnati.	Rev. R.S. Rust, Corresponding Secty, Cincinnati.
Erastus Cravath, Field Supt., Middle Department.	Prof. John Ogden, Agent and Superintendent of Education.

---

societies and the Freedmen's Bureau were common. See Butchart, *Northern Schools, Southern Blacks*, 104-107 and Drake, "American Missionary Assn.," 52, 55-58. The WFAC in effect merged itself into the AMA when the WFAC board voted on 11 March 1870 to discontinue operations and turn over to the other aid society its Cincinnati property and work. *American Missionary*, 14:5 (May 1870): 112.

[75] His title at Fisk varied casually depending upon local perceptions. See Ogden to Tennessee Asst. Commissioner, 11 Sep, 7 Dec, and 30 Dec 1867, 28 Sep and 24 Oct 1868, Letters Received, #7, #12, #15, #16, #7, pp. 340-341, 229, BRFAL, RG 105, NA (M999, BRFAL, Roll 6, pp. 340-341, 229, #7, #12, #15, #16, #7). By 1868 Ogden called himself "Principal, and President Board of Trustees." See Broadside, 4 April 1868, H9318, AMA, Amistad. In 1871 the AMA called Ogden "President of the Board of Trustees." See *Twenty-Fifth Annual Report of the American Missionary Association* (New York, 1871), 38. One source claims that no one had the title of President of the institution before 1875. See Merriam, *Higher Ed. in Tennessee*, 265.

[76] Letter H9092A, 21 April 1866, AMA, Amistad. Even the AMA said at this time that Ogden worked for the other organization. "Prof. John Ogden, of the Western Freedmen's Aid Commission . . . will be superintendent" of Fisk School. *Twentieth Annual Report of the American Missionary Association* (New York, 1866), 36-37. Rust is something of a surprise as a WFAC official (a number of his letters to Ogden survive in the AMA archives) because he is better known for subsequent decades of work with the Freedmen's Aid Society of the Methodist Church which was founded in August 1866, after his WFAC period. See Ralph E. Morrow, *Northern Methodism and Reconstruction* (East Lansing, 1956), 162.

One of Ogden's first ideas in Nashville was to establish a "teachers home" as he had in Macon. He wanted to reduce costs and maintain social support among the northern teachers who were essentially blacklisted by Nashville white society. Nothing came of the idea then, although Fisk School subsumed the teacher housing function a few months later. During the autumn of 1865, however, J.M. Walden, Corresponding Secretary for WFAC, hammered Ogden with letters about teachers for Nashville. He lamented that Ogden was giving him only vague "requisitions" for these human supplies, fussed over their housing, and said that WFAC would pay half their rent in Nashville. Cravath meanwhile reiterated that Nashville was to "be borne jointly" by the AMA and WFAC.[77]

Surprisingly, two years before the Freedmen's Bureau, the WFAC, and the AMA arrived in Nashville, the Rev. J.G. McKee, supported by the United Presbyterian Board of Missions to the Freedmen, had begun a smaller educational effort directed at black youths in the city. McKee was there and operating his school when the others came along. The Freedmen's Bureau started in summer 1865, then Ogden came, working for them and for the Western Freedmen's Aid Commission. Next, the AMA, which in the long run had the greatest staying power, appeared in August 1865 when its two efficient agents, Smith, a former Christian Commission secretary, and Cravath, a former Chaplain of the 101st Ohio Infantry, showed up to "prospect" for a school.[78] They found McKee, the Freedmen's Bureau, Ogden, and the WFAC already there.[79] Nashville attracted these organizations because it had a significant black population. A city census of August 1865 counted 10,744 blacks of whom 3,580 were children under fifteen, an attractive place to focus upon Negro education.[80]

---

[77] Ogden to Walden, 26 August 1865; Walden to Ogden, 18 & 20 October 1865; Cravath to Ogden, 20 January 1866; AMA, Amistad.

[78] Merriam, *Higher Ed. in Tennessee*, 261-262. Hopkins, *Life of Fisk*, 111. Another source gives 3 October 1865. See *The City of Nashville* (n.p., c. 1890), 27; see also Phillips, "Bureau in Tennessee," 236, Drake, "American Missionary Assn.," 92, and McKee to J.B. Clark, 15 January 1866, AMA, Amistad.

[79] E.P. Smith's remarks at Dedication of Jubilee Hall, 1 January 1876, in *Fisk University: History, Building* . . . . [copy in Fisk University Library], 39-40. McKee to J.B. Clark, 15 January 1866, AMA, Amistad. Drake, "American Missionary Assn.," 92.

[80] "Census report of colored population in Nashville," W.T. Clarke, Asst. A-G to General Fisk, 10 August 1865, BRFAL, RG 105, NA (M999, BRFAL, Roll 6).

CHAPTER 4
Establishing Fisk in 1865 and Leading It as School and University

All in all, General Fisk, Superintendent Ogden, and the reverends Cravath, Smith, Rust, and McKee cooperated more than they fought. Ogden was soon working with Smith and Cravath to establish Fisk School which the two AMA men seem at first to have understood as a primary school.[81] The group secured shelter in the former Union Army Construction Corps Nashville Hospital—then available for $16,000. It was located in the "Negro district" on Knowles St. (12th Ave.) between Church and Hynes streets, just west of the Chattanooga Depot. Several wooden barracks totaling 16,500 square feet comprised the 1.25 acre site. A high fence surrounded it. Cravath, Smith, and Ogden personally scraped together $4,000 for a down payment, and gave a note and took a mortgage for the rest. The barracks were low, one-story buildings with side porches, with one two-story building.[82]

Smith explained why they had to have their own quarters:

> From the *citizens* [of Nashville] the less you expect the lighter will be your disappointment. They will not countenance Negro teaching in their present temper. They will not rent for Negro schools if they know it. They will not give a home for teachers of colored schools. If they do missionary or educational work in this

---

[81] Hopkins, *Life of Fisk*, 111. McKee cooperated with Ogden on some matters, but did not give up his own school which he later felt that Fisk School overshadowed. See McKee to Rev. Dr. J. B. Clark, Secretary, U.P.B.F.M., 15 January 1866, AMA, Amistad. Such disagreement as there was seems to have been over tuition. McKee charged tuition but Ogden apparently did not at first, even though WFAC policy was that he should whenever possible. Rust to Ogden, 26 January 1866; McKee to Ogden, 3 September 1866, both AMA, Amistad. The two aid societies disagreed about the tuition matter even in 1866 apparently, since Cravath at the opening exercises said publicly that the school was to be free. See *The Nashville Daily Union*, 10 January 1866. By 1870 Fisk University was trying to get students to pay. See Thomas Moran to Ogden, 22 April 1870, AMA, Amistad.

[82] Smith to Strieby, 11 October 1865, AMA, Amistad; Charles E. Röbert, *Nashville and Her Trade for 1870* (Nashville, 1870), 429; *Fisk University News: Jubilee Singers Number*, 2:5 (October 1911): 44; Hopkins, *Life of Fisk*, 111.

country, your teachers and preachers must come prepared in every place of labor to depend upon themselves for every means of living. They bring a *house* along or money to get one on the spot and means to purchase a *site* at least for the erection of a building that will serve for church and school purposes.[83]

Cravath was Ogden's closest collaborator, and wrote many letters for the school (some on Ogden's government letterhead); he was involved in many details, made many arrangements, and withal performed effectively. It appears that cooperation and friendliness predominated in the two men's relationship (though not necessarily in that of their wives when John Ogden showed up the next year with Anna Brewster). After working together several months Cravath addressed Ogden as "Dear Bro. John," a friendlier expression than those usually found in such letters, and sent him casual gossip when Ogden was away traveling.[84]

Whatever the arrangements, Ogden may have felt it would be impossible to add the impending Fisk School duties to those he was already doing, for on 3 November 1865 he tried to resign the Bureau job, writing General Fisk that, "In accordance with the views I expressed to you a few weeks since, I hereby tender my resignation of the office of Superintendent of Education and Freedmen's Schools in the states of Kentucky and Tennessee . . . ." Fisk turned him down, writing on the verso, "Disapproved, services cannot be spared."[85] General Fisk could take such a line since he was not paying Ogden directly in any case, but with the funds he did control Fisk had sufficient leverage to get what he wanted. Ogden did not broach the matter again, so that when Fisk School opened in January 1866 he simply added the superintendent job there to the Freedmen's Bureau position.[86]

General Fisk understood that doing the two jobs well was inefficient or impossible. The following April he wrote to the Western Freedmen's Aid Commission that "I would be pleased to have Prof

---

[83] Smith to Strieby, 11 October 1865, AMA, Amistad.

[84] Cravath to Strieby, 4,11,13 November 1865; Cravath to Ogden, 13,17 April 1866, AMA, Amistad. Beyond the greeting, his letters suggest a cooperative spirit.

[85] Ogden to Fisk, 3 November 1865, AMA, Amistad. Fisk's endorsement, 11 December 1866, Endorsements Sent, p. 180, BRFAL, RG 105, NA (M999, BRFAL, Roll 4, p. 180.)

[86] Thus Joe Richardson oversimplified when he wrote that Ogden resigned the Freedmen's Bureau job to become principal of Fisk. "Fisk University: The First Critical Years," THQ 29:1 (1970): 30.

Ogden's *entire time* and will remunerate him for his services. I must have *some one* entirely devoted to the Educational interests of my District at large. I would like Prof. Ogden for the place." But it was summer before the problem was finally solved.[87]

In 1865 Ogden was referred to as "Reverend" on more than one occasion. During his 1865-1866 Freedmen's Bureau days, though he was no longer an Army officer, he was sometimes called "Lieutenant" and at least once "Captain," a rank higher than any he had held on active duty though that was still small potatoes compared to Fisk's Brevet Major General.[88]

In December 1865 Cravath and Ogden moved into the former Army hospital buildings and made the final preparations for opening Fisk School the next month. Cravath was delighted to have an *office* at last where could keep his paperwork. Mrs. Cravath became matron of the teacher's home. As they were preparing Fisk School for opening, Ogden's salary was $100 per month plus partial expenses. This was not grand because in 1860, before Civil War inflation, he started the Winona job at $117 per month, and $100 per month was less than the prevailing public school principals' salaries in Nashville.[89] In general, as indicated, the AMA and WFAC split the expense of the school, including salaries, but sometimes asked the Freedmen's' Bureau for help with building maintenance or transportation of goods and personnel.[90]

The opening dedication and ceremonies at the Fisk School on 9 January 1866 were reported in varied tones in different Nashville newspapers. The *American Missionary* in its long and informative report published two months later included a large quantity of detailed

---

[87] Fisk to Rust (Cincinnati) 18 April 1866, Letters Sent, 17 March—29 December 1866, 181, BRFAL, RG 105, NA (M999, BRFAL, Roll 3, p. 181).

[88] Timothy Brigham, U.S. Christian Commission, Knoxville, to General Fisk, TN Asst. Commissioner, Letters Received, BRFAL, RG 105, NA (M999, BRFAL, Roll 6); *Twentieth Annual Report of the American Missionary Association* (New York, 1866), 36-37; Thomas Kennedy (WFAC) to Ogden, 22 December 1865, AMA, Amistad.

[89] At Winona Ogden had started at $1,400 per year. "Historical Sketch and Notes," n.p., n.d., 32-34, cited in Larimer, "Evaluation of Ogden,", 13-14. In Nashville in 1866 public school principals earned between $120 and $150 per month; the monetary value of fringe benefits—apparently including housing for Ogden and family—is, however, difficult to evaluate. See *Nashville Daily Press and Times*, 11 April 1866.

[90] Cravath to Samuel Hunt, 27 December 1865; Cravath to Whipple and Strieby, 6 January 1866; Walden (WFAC) to Whipple (AMA) 4 December 1865, AMA, Amistad.

Establishing Fisk 35

information extracted from unnamed Nashville "papers" which one may infer was the sympathetic *Nashville Daily Press and Times*.[91] Under the heading "Tennessee," the *American Missionary* editors provided the longest account now available:

> From the Nashville papers we clip the following deeply interesting facts and extracts from speeches.
> Opening Exercises of the Fisk Freedmen's School in Nashville, Tennessee Speeches of Gov. Brownlow, General Fisk and others.
>
> The building west of the Chattanooga depot, heretofore used as a military hospital, was yesterday formally dedicated as a colored High School, by appropriate addresses by distinguished military and civil gentlemen of this city.
>
> Prof. John Ogden, of the Western Freedmen's Aid Commission, and Rev. E. M. Cravath of the American Missionary Association, will be Superintendents of the institution.
>
> The following figures will give some idea of the extent of the building. The first division is 170 x 20, and divided into 12 rooms. Three wards 200 x 20 extend back, each divided into 4 sections, the rooms being 50 x 20, and two buildings in the rear, 20 x 60. The whole structure is well ventilated from the roof. The rooms are fourteen feet high, plastered and well lighted. There are four hydrants with water and fire pipes extending through the buildings. The courts within the buildings are handsomely sodded, and over [100?] by 60 feet. The whole appearance of the place is very neat and attractive.
>
> A large concourse of teachers and pupils connected with the various colored schools in the city, with a number of distinguished invited guests, Governor Brownlow, Chancellor Lindsley, of the State University, and Superintendent of the City Schools, Senator Bosson, General Fisk, and a goodly number of other civilians and officers, were present to witness the opening of this institution. The band of the 15th U. S. C. I. were present and varied the

---

[91] In 1866 six daily English newspapers appeared in Nashville. The *Nashville Daily Press and Times* was the most racially liberal and therefore the most sympathetic to Fisk School. *The Nashville Daily Union* was probably next in sympathy and carried a decently long account of the opening exercises on 10 January 1866. The *Republican Banner* was all white and Confederate. *The Nashville Dispatch* was similar while the *Nashville Daily Gazette* was on the far right and barely civilized. I have not seen examples of the sixth paper. Fisk School appears in general to have given its printing business to the *Press and Times* Printing Co. See, e.g., receipt for $105 for catalogue printing, 14 August 1868, AMA, Amistad.

exercises by some excellent music.

After prayer by Rev. R. H. Allen, of the Second Presbyterian Church, Rev. E. M. Cravath gave a brief statement of the foundation and objects of the school. The lot was bought and owned by the Western Freedmen's Commission [sic], and the American Missionary Association of New York, and the buildings were secured by General Fisk. The object was to establish a free school for colored children equal to the best in the country. The building when properly furnished would accommodate from 1200 to 1500 pupils. Children would be taught without charge, and the teachers would be among the best in the country. They desired also to train good teachers in the normal department. It was to be a permanent affair, and would be kept up for at least eight months in the year, if good friends in the North kept their pledges. It was called the Fisk school. The name honored the school, and he trusted that the school would honor the name.

Chancellor Lindsley was then introduced, and made a brief and admirable address, which we cannot give at length. He concluded his remarks by saying:

Let the work of elevation still go on, and let all the friends of education and all well-wishers of Tennessee rejoice that here is a nucleus for the spread of truth and knowledge. Let all speedily avail themselves of its benefits. We wish well to the Fisk school, and would say let it stand until its advantages, now confined to a few thousand persons around this city, shall be enjoyed by 275,000 freedmen of Tennesse[e].

Senator Bosson, of White county, said that his mind was deeply impressed by the thought that man was the noblest work of God. How much noble, generous sentiment is shown in this enterprise, for a people just emerged from bondage, and now taking their rank among human beings as freemen! What strange interest has been awakened by friends in distant States in your behalf. Once they felt for you as slaves, and now that you are free the same sympathy comes up with money that you may take your place as enlightened members of the human family. Do you realize this? Do you feel in your hearts that these kind friends realize your condition? Why should people in other States so soon and so freely give their means to improve and develop you[?] Just as you appreciate this sympathy will you realize the importance of responding properly on your part[?]

General Fisk said that he rejoiced he was permitted to stand as godfather at the baptism of a new and a *free* school. He, too, had been led to take a retrospective glance at this own life to-day. Well did he remember when, more than a quarter of a century ago, his poor, widowed mother, in mid-winter, bound him out to an old farmer. He remembered how the farmer sat in his mother's cabin, and how the contract was written by which he was bound out; how he was to be clothed and sent to school; how his bundle was tied up, and how he was put up on the horse, behind the farmer, with his mother's blessing and tears. These children are much better clad that I was at that time. * * * Chancellor Lindsley gave you a good thought. This war terminates not in slavery, but in liberty for all the land. It struck the shackles off from slaves and gave liberty to 4,000,000 of people. And now, while yet in the smoke and flame of battle, before peace has come and brooded o'er the land, we find these generous people of the North coming down, with all these advantages, and giving them to the freemen freely.

But a few months ago, a citizen of Central Tennessee was tied up to a stake and whipped with forty stripes; for what? Because he had taught a class of eight colored boys to read the spelling book. To-day there are no such scene[s] in Tennessee. We meet under this beautiful banner, in the presence of the Governor of this great Commonwealth, to dedicate this institution to virtuous intelligence, and to make it a free school where shall be taught whatsoever things are true, whatsoever things are just, and lovely, and of good report. I thank God that He has put it into the heart of the people to give their money to establish this school; and let me here say, that within the district over which I have supervision, we have to-day nearly 20,000 colored children enjoying educational advantages free.

The times are not now as they used to be. Why, a little time ago, those boys up there in the other room (the band) who have been discoursing such sweet music, were listening to the notes of the horn of the overseer. To-day, thank God, they blow their own horn. [Loud applause]

Governor Brownlow was then introduced, and spoke as follows:

If I were inclined to make a speech, I am happily relieved by the consideration that nothing has been left for me to say; and I rise at your call merely to testify my approval *in toto* of all that you have said and done, and of all you propose to do. * * * Your naming this the Fisk school is a compliment to a meritorious man. And I will be pardoned for saying in the presence of General Fisk, that, if a man less prudent, less kind, less reasonable, and less just, both towards white and colored persons, had been placed at the head of the [Freedmen's] bureau, in this city, it would have proved a failure.

The Governor, by way of encouraging the young of this school to study, very appropriately related his struggles in early life, and his limited aid from a widowed mother, in indigent circumstances.
* * * I can only say by way of admonition and encouragement to the colored friends: Attend your schools; learn to read the word of God, and then learn to love and practice it; and by way of caution and advise [sic] I admonish you, be mild and temperate in your habits and spirit, and your conduct towards white people. As a friend loving this institution and desiring the prosperity of what you have undertaken, I advice [sic] the teachers, male and female, to be exceedingly prudent and cautious, and do nothing offensive to the predominant party here.

You may think it a little strange that I give such counsel. I do so because if General Thomas were to take away his soldiers, and pull up stakes and leave here, you would not be allowed to occupy this school room a week, not a week.

After interesting remarks from Rev. R. H. Allen, Mr. Walker and Rev. Mr. Harris, the two last colored men, Rev. E. M. Cravath arose and announced that the school would be open for pupils at nine o'clock to-morrow. He thanked the friends for their large attendance to-day. The Mayor of the city had offered to lend them a helping hand, and co-operate in the good work. He spoke of the friendly co-operation extended to like enterprises in Macon and Atlanta. His hopes today had been more than fulfilled. The reports of the meeting would go out in the newspapers and encourage the hearts of our friends in the North to increase our funds. It was deeply gratifying to see an official recognition from Tennessee, in the person of her Governor, and from the Superintendent of the city schools of Nashville.

The assembly then dispersed, and the visitors after a brief social conference departed, highly gratified with what they had seen and heard.[92]

---

[92] William G. Brownlow ("Parson" Brownlow), 1805-1877, was an eastern Tennessee newspaper editor and Unionist who served as Governor of Tennessee, 1865-1869, following which he served in the U. S. Senate. William Bosson (1803-1887), was a Unionist born in Massachusetts who lived in Tennessee, 1841-1872, serving in the Tennessee Senate 1865-1867 and the Tennessee House, 1867-1869, J. B. Lindsley was Superintendent of Nashville public schools in 1866 and was sometimes referred to as "Chancellor of the University."

The report of the opening in *The Nashville Daily Union* (preceded the day before with a coyly-worded notice that "[w]e are requested to announce . . . ." the opening and "[w]e would urge all our citizens who feel an interest in the enterprise to attend the exercises to-day"), was not as long as the report quoted above; decently polite, it contained slightly different but complementary information, leading one to surmise that the *American Missionary* editors had picked and chosen what to report from the Nashville "papers." *The Daily Union* report, right at the top as part of the heading, proclaimed "The Governor Still Belligerent," a typical statement that Confederate sympathizers and anti-Reconstructionists made about Brownlow for a century. Beyond that, however, the *Daily Union* report was straightforward and provided some information suppressed or ignored by the American Missionary Association staff in New York. The *Daily Union* quoted Cravath as saying that the Fisk School would open "at first as a sort of High School and afterwards, if circumstances are favorable, [the buildings] are to be used as a college." This shows the ultimate goal that Cravath, at least (Ogden did not speak at the opening exercises), had for the institution. Apparently bowing, however, to the silent Ogden, Cravath also stated that ". . . a feature of the school will be the instruction of those who wish to become teachers."[93] Cravath's state-ments were remarkable in stating two hopes or goals that were actually fulfilled in the decades and the century following. Among the many insti-tutions that stated lofty goals but failed to reach them, these sober and carefully phrased remarks, made the day the school opened, stand out.

Symbolic of the barriers, however, another part of the Nashville press commented that week too, and with pronounced hostility. The *Nashville Daily Gazette* said:

Sambo Still Ahead
On Tuesday somewhere about the R.R. Depot, there was a jollification, upon opening of "Fisk Freedmen's School." Of course the opportunity for speech-making and self-display was not

---

[93] *The Nashville Daily Union*, 9 and 10 January 1866. Cravath's mention of the normal function was not the first I have found. On 8 August 1865, General Fisk, speaking before the "Convention of the Colored People of the State" in the St. John's Chapel A.M.E. Church in Nashville had said, "I propose also a good normal school for the education of colored teachers." Fisk's remarks were quite radical; he literally mentioned "forty acres, with tools, mules...." *The Colored Tennessean* 1:16 (12 August 1865).

> allowed to pass unimproved. The Rev. E. M. Cravath, (Cravat!) superintendent Lindsley, . . . Gen. Fisk, . . . successively occupied the rostrum and, for aught we know, electrified the audience. Some audiences are easily electrified.[94]

This too was part of the environment in which Ogden and Cravath began superintending the new school.

Within of month or so of the opening of the school problems arose concerning the passage of the students back and forth between home and school. The earliest mention seems to be a "paper" from Miss E. A. Easter, a teacher at Fisk, to the American Missionary Association. Much of her statement, sent with a cover letter from Cravath and intended for publication in the *American Missionary*, somewhat sentimentally recounted the ardent desire of the freedpeople to learn to read the Scriptures, but she also testified that

> These children experience many difficulties in coming to school for the white children are so incensed at the thought of niggers *learning to read* that they often stone them on their way to and from school. My own scholars have had some sad experiences in this direction. I myself have several times acted as a Guard for these poor children. One of the teachers here in this city has applied for a guard to protect school children on their way to and from school.
> Those that *teach* these colored people are not exempt from these manifestations of disgust and hatred.[95]

Nearly a month later, 8 March, as the problem was apparently still not resolved, Ogden and J. G. McKee jointly wrote General Fisk. They variously described the activities as white boys stoning black boys, or a mutual stoning, and asked,

> Can anything be done by the Military or Civil Authorities of Nashville to put a stop to the disgraceful mobs of boys, white and black, that throng the alleys and byways, west of the Chattanooga Depot, throwing stones and other missiles at each other, to the

---

[94] *Nashville Daily Gazette*, 12 January 1866, probably written by Edwin Paschall, Political Editor.

[95] Miss E. A Easter to AMA, 12 February 1866, AMA, Amistad.

> danger and destruction of life and property and property of peaceable citizens?
>
> Already complaints have been make to us of the destruction of property; and our pupils are almost daily assailed on their way to and from School, and frequently are cut and bruised to an alarming extent.[96]

The clerk's paraphrase of the incoming letter ran "Asks that steps be take to prevent boys from throwing stones. A number of his pupils assailed daily." Whatever was done in response was apparently insufficient because three weeks later J. G. McKee wrote again and the Clerk's statement of the "purport" of his letter was that "Supt. McKee . . . reports ill-conduct of white boys and asks for their arrest." Ogden and McKee, from their positions, tended to see their own pupils as the beleaguered in this particular strife. General Fisk, taking the higher political view that men in his position tend to do, compromised by ordering ten of each color arrested and punished.[97]

The Fisk School in the cheaply constructed former Army hospital barracks in downtown Nashville was always a marginal operation—in financing, equipment, maintenance, and safety. Although the school began operation in January 1866, two months later Ogden was still requesting from General Fisk's office "transportation for school furniture" and "a clerk to assist." Late that year Cravath beseeched the Tennessee Freedmen's Bureau Assistant Commissioner—General Fisk being gone by that time—for school desks and building repairs. The next year he asked for modifications and repairs to the school. In 1868 the Board asked for repairs and improvements in the large sum (for the day) of $9,254.00, which request the Assistant Commissioner declined, saying that as the present year's appropriation was only $25,000 he could not grant the request, but that "the D.O. will make such repairs as necessary to preserve the buildings already in use," implying that it was questionable if the structures would remain usable unless they received serious maintenance.[98]

---

[96] Ogden and McKee to General Fisk, 8 March 1866, AMA, Amistad.

[97] *American Missionary*, 9:4 (April 1866): 88-89. Ogden [and McKee?] to Fisk, 8 March 1866, #18, BRFAL, RG 105, NA (M999, BRFAL, Roll 5, p. 286, #18). McKee to Fisk, 29 March 1866, #90, BRFAL, RG 105, NA (M999, BRFAL, Roll 5, p. 248, #90).

[98] Ogden to Fisk, 9, 10 February, 2 March 1866, Letters Rec'd, nos. 8, 11, 17; Cravath to BRFAL Tenn. Asst. Commissioner, 22 October 1866, Letters Rec'd, #139; all BRFAL,

The advent of summer 1866 marked the conclusion of the academic year and for Ogden, the staff, the board, and the students it was a breathing time and a taking-stock time. Year-end reports were supposedly written, successes calculated, plans laid for the following year, and most of the faculty traveled northward to see familiar terrain, visit families, and in Ogden's case, get married. As the first term closed on 15 June 1866 Ogden reported that nearly 1,000 students had been registered and he had fifteen teachers on the faculty; as agent of the WFAC he paid them off that day.[99]

Ogden finished a demanding year bearing two titles—"Superintendent" of Fisk School and "Superintendent" of Education for the Freedmen's Bureau in Tennessee; neither was hollow. For example, in March 1866 he visited Memphis and in April 1866, wearing his Freedmen's Bureau hat, he was in Covington and Cynthiana, Kentucky, establishing schools; in the same month he visited Lexington, Louisville, and Cincinnati.[100]

Thus unsurprisingly, after the final school exercises in mid-June 1866 Ogden wasted no time heading north. Within a week Cravath wrote him in Ohio saying that he was enclosing what he thought would be a welcome letter, and elaborating, "I think the Societies [the Western Freedmen's Aid Commission and the American Missionary Association] will arrange to make you the Principal of the Fisk School for the coming year. This I understand to be on the whole your preference. Gen. Fisk will then get a new man on his staff." The letter he enclosed, what we would today call a position description, not only implicitly offered Ogden the Principalship, but also seemed to try to regulate the top administration of the Fisk School. In full, it read, to no addressee:

> The undersigned Com[mitt]ee on the Fisk School agree upon the following general plan for the School year beginning Sept. 1st,

---

RG 105, NA (M999, BRFAL, Roll 5, pp. 285, 71.) Cravath to same, 2 October 1867, Letters Rec'd, #124; Tennessee Assistant Commissioner [?] to O. O. Howard [?], 25 August 1868, #128, BRFAL, RG 105, NA (M999, BRFAL, Roll 6, pp. 79, 159.)

[99] Ogden married Anna Brewster 16 August 1866. *American Missionary*, 10:8 (August 1866): 184.

[100] Ogden to Fisk, 23 April 1866, Letters Received, #27, BRFAL, RG 105, NA (M999, BRFAL, Roll 5, p. 287, #27). Fisk to Ogden, 25 April 1866, Letters Sent, p. 240, BRFAL, RG 105, NA (M999, BRFAL, Roll 3, p. 240). Rev. T.C. Bliss to AMA, 3 March 1866; Ogden letters, 13, 18, 25 April 1866, all AMA, Amistad.

1866, and ending July 1st 1867 to wit—

1. There shall be a Steward in general charge of the buildings and the school and house furniture and the table supplies, and all family or financial affairs of the school. Who shall keep all appropriate money accounts and make a monthly report to this Com[mitt]ee. The salary for this office shall be $50 per month and all expenditures of board washing fuel and lights not including handing expenses. If necessary for the Steward to remain thro' the year of 12 months his salary shall continue for the whole 12 months at the same rate.

2. There shall be a principal teacher who shall have a school room and devote his time to classes and take general supervision of the other teachers assigning them rooms, and pupils and recitations. This teacher shall give at least five hours per day to this work in the School and make such monthly reports of the number and progress of the pupils and the General Condition of the School as the Com[mitt]ee may desire. his salary shall be $100 per month for the ten months and expense of board, washing, fuel and light—not including handling expense—

Signed   Edwd P. Smith
                M. Sawyer
                R. S. Rust[101]

General Fisk wrote Ogden about the same time saying that he had conferred with Smith and Cravath and they had concluded that Ogden ought to move over to Fisk School full time so as to "give it all your time, energy and admirable adaptability." Fisk added that he would look for an education superintendent replacement in the Freedmen's Bureau. The General may have regretted his words of praise because a few days later he wrote Ogden to say that he was "quite annoyed" that Ogden had left town before completing the year-end school reports, adding that General Howard, the Freedmen's Bureau commander in Washington, "is very desirous that the Report should be in early in this month." Fisk was a short-timer himself, for President Andrew Johnson wanted a more malleable man in the Tennessee job, perhaps someone less self-confident

---

[101] Cravath to Ogden, 23 June 1866; The Smith, Sawyer, and Rust committee letter is not adjacent to the Cravath letter in the microfilmed archive, but the text quoted is found a bit later, headed "Copy," and dated 10 July 1866, AMA, Amistad. Changes could have been negotiated between 23 June and 10 July, since all the principals were in or near Cincinnati during that period, but in all likelihood the 10 July 1866 copy is the statement that Cravath sent to Ogden.

who would support the Freedmen less articulately that Fisk did. President Johnson ordered the Secretary of War to fire Fisk and put someone else in. That was done in spite of General Howard's resistance, and Fisk was mustered out on 18 August 1866 to take effect 1 September 1866.[102]

General Fisk was recognized and thanked prominently as he was to leave Nashville. A letter of thanks appeared in the paper and he was invited to speak at the State Capitol. The proceedings at the Capitol and his speech there were prominently reported on the front page of the *Daily Press and Times*. Among other recognitions, the colored ladies of Nashville presented a silver service to Mrs. Fisk.[103]

Later that year, away from Nashville, General Fisk continued to speak up for the Fisk School. The *American Missionary* reported somewhat self-interestedly that in an address at Williamsburgh, New York (as reported in the New York *Tribune*), "this distinguished and admirable officer" made the following remarks:

> The American Missionary Association had done more (in his department) than all others for the education of the Freedmen. He loved to speak of that honored institution, to which he trusted the people of Williamsburgh would give $10,000 or $15,000 as a Christmas present. At Nashville the "Fisk School" for Freedmen had been established by that Society. Thousands of children were there being taught as well as in any school in the country. He had visited many schools in his lifetime but never a better one that this, nor did he ever see greater progress by pupils than was there being made. He never, in any other school, saw such a hungering and thirsting after knowledge.[104]

During the summer of 1866 Ogden and Cravath had taken the initiative in suggesting to General Fisk who ought—and ought not—to replace Ogden in the Tennessee education superintendency. Cravath

---

[102] Fisk to Ogden, 10 July 1866, AMA, Amistad; Fisk to Ogden, 6 July 1866 and 10 July 1866, Letters Sent (17 March-29 December 1866), pp. 491 and 494, BRFAL, RG 105, NA (M999, BRFAL, Roll 3, pp. 491, 494); Hopkins, *Life of Fisk*, 126; General Howard to General Fisk, 13 September 1866, Howard Papers, Letters Sent, cited in George R. Bentley, *A History of the Freedmen's Bureau* (New York, 1974; first pub. 1955), 244, n. 78.

[103] *The Nashville Daily Press and Times*, 1 and 3 September 1866.

[104] *American Missionary*, 10:12 (December 1866): 274.

Establishing Fisk

wrote from Winona, Minnesota, reporting that "Prof. Spence is not a suitable person for Supt. of Education."[105] While Adam K. Spence four years later did succeed Ogden as President of Fisk University and served five years in that role with apparent satisfaction, the job of state Education Superintendent in the Freedmen's Bureau differed considerably from administering one school. Cravath may well have been correct in believing that Spence would not be effective in the Freedmen's Bureau school superintendency. It was rough and ready work, requiring travel to small towns and effective interpersonal skills to deal successfully on the spot with resentful white Southerners.

Ogden had a strong conception of what it took to be effective. He did not care for confrontation and on the back of an incoming letter from a subagent in Maury County who reported with bitterness the burning of a schoolhouse, Ogden drafted the following, perhaps to Cravath:

> I am satisfied that Mears [the subagent] is not a proper man to go among the people—the best radicals of Maury tell me he is not. You could go down to Mt. Pleasant and get the *Secesh* to build a school house. Mears deals in antagonisms, I don't like him for the business.[106]

Ogden himself may not have been as effective in the Freedmen's Bureau educational superintendency as his successor who appears to have done more in the position than Ogden had. On the same day that Cravath ruled out Spence, Ogden recommended the Reverend David Burt of Winona, Minnesota, to succeed him in the Freedmen's Bureau position. Ogden knew Burt personally from Winona days because Burt had served on the "Prudential Committee" of the Minnesota Normal School. General Fisk, or the man who followed him, accepted the recommendation and Burt went to Tennessee to succeed Ogden. To judge from the quantity and detail of Burt's correspondence to the Assistant Commissioner over the next two years, Ogden found a good man in Burt who got around the state, oversaw the territory, and submitted many requests for the repair and upkeep of school buildings.[107]

---

[105] Cravath to Fisk, 6 August 1866, Letters Rec'd, #132, BRFAL, RG 105, NA (M999, BRFAL, Roll 5, p. 70, #132).

[106] Mears (Columbia, TN) to Ogden, 14 October 1865, AMA, Amistad.

[107] Ogden to Fisk, Letters received, #32; BRFAL, RG 105, NA (M999, BRFAL, Roll 5, p.

In 1866 the normal-school question—training blacks to become teachers in the South—moved to the top of the agenda for the boards of the Northern aid organizations. Fisk was just starting as a primary school or graded school, but the officers of the AMA in New York were thinking that it was unduly expensive to send white Northern teachers South to staff primary schools, and that a more effective strategy would be to keep a relatively small number of trained and experienced white teachers there, use them to instruct lower-paid young black men and women for common school teaching jobs and thereby multiply the power of their funds.[108]

The American Missionary Association Executive Committee formally took such a decision shortly after 31 May 1866, in advance of the Freedmen's Bureau's adoption of the same policy. The *American Missionary* reported that

> At a conference of a few friends and officers of the American Missionary Association, in Boston, May 31st, 1866, the subject of Normal Schools being considered, it was
>
> "Resolved, That we regard it as a matter of the highest importance that the Executive officers of the American Missionary Association should give their earnest attention to the organization of Normal Schools, and to their speedy advancement of the highest state of perfection."
>
> . . . . This recommendation was subsequently laid before the Executive Committee of the A. M. A. and approved.
>
> That there is an immense work to be done for the education of the masses of the colored people of the South, far beyond what can be accomplished by the direct labor of teachers sent from the North, cannot be doubted. Much of it, for various reasons, must be done by teachers raised up from among the people themselves. The Executive Committee of this Association has already entered upon the work of supplying this want, and, deeply impressed with its importance, will endeavor to carry out the view of the conference referred to. To do this will require, for a short time, larger expenditures than on the ordinary primary schools; but, in

---

287, #32.) Burt to Assistant Commissioner, Letters Received, *passim*, 1866-1868, BRFAL, RG 105, NA (M999, BRFAL, Rolls 4-6). Neill and Ogden, *Addresses Delivered*, 2.

[108] Beard, *Crusade of Brotherhood*, 147-149; Joe M. Richardson, *Christian Reconstruction: The American Missionary Association and Southern Blacks, 1861-1890* (Athens, GA: University of Georgia Press, 1986), 109-113.

Establishing Fisk

the end, the best economy will be reached, as in many places, schools under these colored teachers will in a short time become self-sustaining.[109]

The Board of Fisk School and John Ogden, according to Cravath's report in the *American Missionary*, implemented the decision right away so that at the start of the fall term on 3 September 1866 Fisk opened as "a thoroughly graded school with a normal class . . . and the third day four hundred pupils were present." Cravath also said that "the Principal, Prof. Ogden, is a teacher of large experience with Normal schools," that he had taken the matter firmly in hand in Nashville, and that normal classes would also be offered in other important Southern cities.[110]

The 3 September 1866 reported starting date for normal training at Fisk was later contradicted by Ogden himself. Writing in 1868 to Rev. George Whipple at the American Missionary Association Ogden said that "its [Fisk's] most distinct characteristic has been from the beginning, [to be] a Normal or Training school for colored teachers." This statement seems flatly in error, for Fisk did not begin in January 1866 as a normal school; Ogden went on to develop the contradiction even further and placed the start of normal training *even later* than Cravath did; Ogden claimed that the first normal class of twelve was organized in November, 1867, the second normal class of ten in January, 1868, and that both groups were teaching in the model school.[111] There is no easy way to reconcile these statements. One can only surmise that at different times Ogden had different ways of thinking about what constituted a proper normal school, or a normal "class."

During these years he also considered from time to time the possibility that the state government of Tennessee would finance public

---

[109] *American Missionary*, 10: 8 (August, 1866): 190.

[110] Drake, "American Missionary Association," 159-160; Cravath, report on "Middle Dept.," *American Missionary*, 10:10 (October 1866): 217-218.

[111] Ogden to George Whipple, 29 February 1868, AMA, Amistad. Adding to the confusion, Ogden received a "lot" of his own normal-school textbook, *The Science of Education* at Nashville as early as November 1865. Moore, Wilstach & Baldwin to Ogden, 27 November 1865, AMA, Amistad. Their only possible use was for teacher education, but A.A. Taylor said that when Fisk School opened in January 1866 no student "had gone beyond the fifth reader, rudimentary arithmetic, and elementary grammar." "Fisk University and the Nashville Community, 1866-1900," *Journal of Negro History*, 39:2 (April 1954): 113.

education and that that would increase the demand for trained black teachers for public schools. In May 1867, he wrote that "my opinion is that schools like this one [Fisk] in Tenn. ought to be fashioned into normal schools as soon as possible. I think the primary school, at least in large cities, will be supported by the state, which will make a larger demand for colored teachers." He pursued the theme six months later, stressing the revenue that Fisk could generate by providing such training; he told Smith that he thought the state of Tennessee was going to spend some money on normal schools and that Fisk could get some of it if they went to a normal school format.[112]

Ogden dreamed of money not only from the state of Tennessee, but also from the Peabody Education Fund, managed by the peripatetic Dr. Barnabas Sears, who influenced Ogden at this time. In November 1867 Sears had visited Fisk and been satisfied enough with that he saw to send Ogden $800 to help support sixteen of the most promising Negro education students Ogden could locate in Tennessee. Sears's opinions correlated with Ogden's on school format: both preferred normal schools over normal departments in colleges and academies. Sears believed that in the latter cases the normal departments would "be overshadowed by the literary and scientific departments, and fail to win the regards and excite the enthusiasm or students or the interest of the general public."[113]

The Fisk School Board of Trustees resolution to inaugurate normal training in 1866—no matter when the training actually began—was an interim decision because the following year the board determined to raise Fisk to university status just as Cravath had suggested in his remarks at the January 1866 opening ceremonies. The understood purpose of Fisk when it had been in the planning stages in the autumn of 1865 seems to have been to provide primary instruction to freedmen in Nashville.[114]

---

[112] Ogden to E.P. Smith (New York), 8 May 1867, 25 November 1867, AMA, Amistad.

[113] Ogden to Whipple, 29 February 1868, AMA, Amistad. Sear's 1868 report, cited in J.L.M. Curry, *A Brief Sketch of George Peabody, and a History of the Peabody Education Fund Through Thirty Years*, (New York, 1969; first pub. 1898), 39. The Peabody Fund worked in the South, gave two-thirds of its money to white schools but gave each black school *per capita* only two-thirds as much as white schools. Ogden to Tenn. Asst. Commissioner., Ltrs Rec'd, #7, 18 March 1867, BRFAL, RG 105, NA (M999, BRFAL, Roll 6, p. 227, #7). William B. Vaughn, *Schools for All: The Blacks and Public Education in the South, 1865-1877* (Lexington, 1974), 144-146; McPherson, *Abolitionist Legacy*, 148.

[114] "Remarks of E.P. Smith at Services of Dedication [of Jubilee Hall]," 1 January 1876 in

During John Ogden's first two years as head, the Board of Trustees went beyond that and decided that the institution would not only provide normal training, but would aspire to university status. The Trustees had choices: Fisk could become a university and offer college-level work to a few; it could become a normal school and train relatively large numbers of teachers for the common and graded schools of Tennessee; or it could remain a school in Nashville—serving as an elementary school or a high school with normal classes.

When Ogden joined the discussion of Fisk's role, he by experience and education thought that the teacher-training function ought to take priority. A teacher years later described Ogden in Nashville as a man "whose chief joy was the preparation of teachers." But the chief joy of the Board of Trustees lay elsewhere, and it resolved that beginning in 1867 Fisk School would be Fisk University.[115] In spite of the decision, however, no college-level instruction was offered until 1871, after Ogden was gone. That could have resulted from stalling on his part, but more likely it came from the simple unavailability of students to do the higher-level work. The teacher quoted above said that even the "most advanced students [in 1869-1870] were not beyond the first year of the ordinary high school." This was common throughout the nation, and Fisk University, along with many other institutions called "colleges" or "universities," continued for decades to provide a lower-level preparatory school that had nothing directly to do with its higher education mission. Ogden himself was not opposed to that type of mixed-school organization because in 1860 at Winona he had described such a combination as ideal. Not only did preparatory work continue in the 1870s when Fisk began functioning as a university, but teacher training too, because it could not then be left aside, the need at all levels being so great.[116]

Tennessee and the Freedmen needed normal schools immediately and would need universities within a few years. Over the long run, Fisk

---

Fisk University: History, Buildings, cited in Hopkins, *Life of Fisk*, 111.

[115] Fisk was "incorporated [as a university] under the laws of Tennessee, August 22, 1867, with a board of nine trustees." American Missionary Association, *History of the American Missionary Association* (New York, 1891), 27.

[116] Helen C. Morgan, "Fisk University Before the Jubilee Singers Went Forth," *Fisk University News*, 2:5 (October 1911): 15-16. The long-continued prep work at Fisk tends to substantiate Ogden's view that Tennessee needed a broader educational base before attention went to higher education. Ogden, in Neill and Ogden, *Addresses Delivered*, 26.

University would almost certainly have evolved to its present form no matter which course the Board of Trustees elected in 1867 because virtually all teacher-training colleges have become general colleges or universities since 1945. And while normal school or "school of education," faculty fall into a group that intellectuals have sternly criticized since the 1950s, there was a time when normal schools and normal-school careers commanded respect, when serious people believed that teacher training posed demands, and when men (and many women) unafraid of intellectual challenges sought normal-school careers. But the prestige that normal-school training once possessed has faded and virtually all such schools have striven to become universities.[117]

The Board decision to move to university status was a reasonable choice that has endured. But given Ogden's normal-school interests and background his departure a few years later from the Fisk University presidency is unsurprising.

---

[117] A recent example, among many, is Jurgen Herbst, *And Sadly Teach: Teacher Education and Professionalism in American Education* (Madison, 1989).

CHAPTER 5
Students, Chapels and Churches

Since Ogden's principal claim upon our attention is his leadership of an early black school that evolved into an institution of higher learning, how did he function in the role and what were his relationships with the students? It appears that black students liked him and enjoyed the Fisk environment. Letters from July 1868 from students at home for the summer expressed a variety of feelings and concerns:

>Memphis Tenn July 1, 1868
>Dear teacher I arrived safely yesterday at 9 o'clock and we had a very pleasant time on the way and we find times very dull here and also very warm. I would like to know how much you would charge for my sister she is about 12 years old and is a very bright little scholar. I will devote my time in study when I am not at work. I have not any employment yet. I will bring letter to a close. forgive my mistakes if you plese I do my best this is a very short letter but when a body dont know much they cant write much. your obedient servant Thomas Mason.

>Memphis Tenn July 2, 1868
>Mr. Ogden
>Dear teacher after two days meditation of our sad departure from your School I have concluded to write you a few lines to inform you of our arrival home we arrived home safe on the 30 and are now well and getting along very well and I am going to Stard a School at home next Monday.
> Give My respects to all the Teachers and Students
> I remain your Obedient Student   Fred Hunt

>Memphis Tenn July 6th, 68
>Mr Ogden
>   Dear Sir
>I arrived safely home on Thursday morning I can assure you that we were greeted by many friends I found my Mother in very poor health but the rest of the family was well and doing well I spent the Sabbath very happy. I attended Sabbath School I have a class of little boys' I like them very much I am going to try to teach

them the best I can although I dont know very much I feel glad that I got the opportunity of going to school for I was very much benefeited by going I learned more in my books' than I ever knew and more than all I learned of my Dear Saviour I don't entend to stop trying to serve him as long as I live I hope to come back next fall if my Mother can spare me I know she will if posible although she has very poor health and cant do very well with out me Emma is well and sends her love to you and Mrs Ogden and kiss little Johnnie for her give my love all of the Teachers on the grounds' Mattie and the rest of the Scholars are well I saw them last evening times are very hard and business dull I dont think there is much sickness in the city the weather is very warm and the streets are very dusty. we had a very nice shower this evening which was needed very much give my love to Mr and Mrs. Bennett also Mr and Mrs White and Mrs Aery [Aray] So I will close asking you to please excuse bad writing and spelling
    from your dear pupil
      Alice A Allen

    Murfreesboro, Tenn.
     July 6th / 68
Proff. Jno Ogden,
  My kind fried [sic] according to promise, I will try to scribble you a letter. There is not much chance of getting a school here as I can learn, but I was down to Woodberry yesterday and learned that the prospect of two schools are very good, (but to my dissatisfaction as time is so precious with me,) I cannot obtain confident satisfaction untill Wensday evening. I would like very much to hear from you soon and have your advise what to do, as I am somewhat perplexed just now. I am now at the house of a friends of mine about a mile from town.
Give my love to all my friends
Write *soon* if you *will* for I feel lonesome indeed.
Yours most Obedient
   Jno. H. Burrows

    Memphis Tenn July 8th 1868
Mr Ogden Dear Sir
  I arrived safe home on Tuesday and all my friend was very very glad to see me and was glad to hear that I was so pleased with the school. We are ready to come back now we have seen our friends we all expect to come back and bring as many more with

us Mother and Father are very happy to know that Pam is pleased with the school they are very much oblige to you for your kindness and Pam also. Give my love all my teachers that is their and to Emma and kiss the baby for me. Ma and Pa wishes to be remmembered to you from your Dear scholar Fannie Pearl[118]

Two years later another absent student complimented Ogden in passing but this student's letter is perhaps more important in that it touches upon some of the typical concerns expressed in student letters—getting back to the school, being sufficiently prepared for the studies, bringing other students along, and paying the fees.

> Chattanooga Tennessee
> Aug. 11th, 1870.
>
> Dear Sir,
>   Prof. Ogden
> It is with pleasure that I seat myself down this after noon to write you a few lines to inform you that I am well at this time present, and hope these few lines may find you in better health than I heard you were in. I thought I would come up to School the 1st of October, to stay one session, with you in School. I would have come last year but was not quite ready, but I think I shall be ready, by the first of October. Some of the other boys want to come too. I all ways thought a great deal of you, and when I come I expect to sign for two (2) or three (3) years. I would like to know from you ll [sic] what the charges are in the Grammar School and high school, next year. I see Isaac has made a great improvement in his studies since he has been up to your school nothing more at present.
>   Respectfully Yours
>   Augustus Hawkins[119]

Many white teachers and colleagues, *if* they were not too puritanical, seemed also to like Ogden. He was witty at times, but flippant—too much so for many people who considered him unduly friendly and familiar with students in an age when faculty were often imperious. The Rev. E.O. Tade, a rigid colleague in Chattanooga, cast aspersions on Ogden that have been several times repeated. Writing to E.P. Smith, he said:

---

[118] Letters H 9346a, H 9347a, H 9347b, H 9347c, and H 9349a, AMA, Amistad.

[119] Augustus Hawkins to Ogden, 11 August 1870, AMA, Amistad.

Superintendent Ogden in the first place is not a real gentleman, and in the second place has a poor moral reputation, and in the third place he says "I am a Methodist all over" & in the fourth place he acts just as if he thought bro. Mullery was not needed about the Fisk school.

And then besides all this only one teacher in the whole institution seemed to have any sympathy for him or his work—all this I saw without being told anything, then bro. Mullery confirmed it all & more too. He asked me to write of these things. Now what is the use of keeping Ogden in that position! I don't want it but I can name more than a dozen who can fill it better than he does. Is it right for a Supt. to *chuck* young ladies under the chin—and especially for a man who wooed & won his present wife while a school girl & that too when his first wife was living? What can the religious influence of such a man be?

Ogden's successful pursuit of the young Gussie Brewster (eighteen years his junior) at Winona had come back to cause him mild trouble. Had Tade known that Ogden's first wife was not only not dead but not even divorced from him when he first met Miss Brewster at Winona in 1861, and still neither dead nor divorced from him when Ogden resumed contact with Miss Brewster after the war, Tade would have been even more shocked.[120]

But less than a year later Tade either was hiding his feelings from Ogden because Fisk School offered something that Tade wanted for his students, or Tade had changed his mind and became something of a convert and enthusiast for Fisk School, for he now was writing as follows:

       Chattanooga Tenn
         Feb 29th 1868

Prof John Ogden
Fisk Unist. Nashville, Tenn.

---

[120] Tade to E.P. Smith, 8 and 15 May 1867, AMA, Amistad. In the first letter he said that he had visited Nashville in February and had also subsequently made inquiries. The Rev. W. W. Mullery is a man whose Nashville role I have not identified. He first appears in the AMA correspondence in October 1866 writing to Whipple from Nashville on matters pertaining to his recent AMA-authorized move to that city. He seems not to have served on the Fisk faculty. An obvious inference that could be drawn from Tade's statements is that Ogden had let it be understood—perhaps implied—that his first wife was dead. For him she apparently was, but anyone listening to his words might have taken them in a literal sense.

> Dear Friend
>
> I have been talking with two of my best boys—told them that they must be examined in the fundamental rules of Arithmetic. They think they are ready for that—the next question was the means—I urged them to raise $15 each towards board—if they can do that can they both come. They are both together in their studies
>
> They would like to be together if possible. They are both members of our Church & I have no fears but they will quit themselves well if we can but get them fairly harnessed in.
>
> If they go *now* is a good time to become interested & acquainted at the Fisk.
>
> Suppose they can raise each $15 will that & the Peabody pay Board & washing?
>
> Yours, with kind regards to all
> E. O. Tade[121]

This was just an opener; several times in the following years Tade tried to arrange for his better students to go to Nashville and study in Ogden's school.

Some whites, perhaps slightly puritanical, but with a streak of the "cleanliness is Godliness" attitude, admired Ogden. Helen Morgan, a teacher of Latin and one of the ablest members of the Fisk faculty for nearly a half-century beginning in 1869 observed that "with Professor Ogden cleanliness and order were cardinal virtues."[122]

Ogden also got into minor trouble during his later years at Fisk because some critics thought that he did not show enough interest in the construction of a church building—which turned out to be Howard Chapel, opened 1869—on the Fisk campus. While by most standards Ogden would appear to have been quite an intense Christian, his alleged lukewarmness on church construction—coupled with the fact that he, sometimes considered a Methodist (as Tade's letter made clear), was looked upon as an outsider in the heavily Congregationalist AMA—led to a certain amount of sniping. The gossip that he was not interested in

---

[121] Tade to Ogden, 29 February 1868; also 3 October 1868 and several subsequent letters, the last noted from John E. Patton, 24 August 1870: "I am one of E O Tade's scholars." All AMA, Amistad.

[122] Helen C. Morgan, "Fisk University Before the Jubilee Singers Went Forth," *Fisk University News*, 2:5 (October 1911), 14-15. McPherson, *Abolitionist Legacy*, 171.

5. John Ogden, ca. 1892. Courtesy of Mary Lee Grenfell Shelton, an Ogden descendant.

6. John Ogden's second wife, Anna Brewster Ogden (1842-1908), 1858. Courtesy of Mary Lee Grenfell Shelton.

the chapel building is not borne out by his correspondence. He positively exulted to E. P. Smith in describing the 40 x 80 foot brick Howard Chapel and said that "we have the best Chapel south of the Ohio river."[123]

But in the previous year Ogden had been very touchy about whether a church then being founded in Nashville (whether situated

---

[123] Ogden to Smith, 15 February 1869, AMA, Amistad.

physically on Fisk School property or not I cannot tell) was a union church (all creeds) or a Congregational church. The differing views gave rise to a forceful correspondence between, on the one hand, Ogden and those of the Fisk staff in whose name he spoke, and the AMA staff in New York on the other hand. Although Ogden strongly desired that the Fisk faculty and staff side be published in the *American Missionary*, it apparently never was. The correspondence, though we generally have Ogden's side only, is easy to follow in spite of his occasionally tangled syntax.

Nashville, Tenn. June 28th 1868
Dear Brethren [of the A.M.A. staff]

Having noticed a statement in the *American Missionary* of this month copied from the *Congregationalist*, to the effect that a Congregational Church had been established in Nashville, and supposing it to refer to the independent "Union Church," organized a few months since in this place, we, the teachers and friends of the A.M.A. & W.F.A.C. representing four or five different religious denominations, beg leave to make the following statement in order to correct what we regard as an unintentional error.

1. Engaged as we are, in the education and religious training of Colored people, and believing that we could accomplish both these objects better were we to unite in an independent Church organization, where each individual of us could be allowed to retain, if so desired, not only our own peculiar religious tenets but our present Church connections, and thus unite all our strength in an independent Church organization for the purpose of enticing the Colored people in a more harmonious and consistent effort for their elevation, we did organize ourselves into what is known as the "Union Church of Nashville."

2. We also state that it was clearly and distinctly understood by all, that the organization would not be denominational, nor *necessarily* Congregational, unless its members, at any subsequent time, should so vote it.

It was voted unanimously on the day of organization, 1st that the object desired in organizing this Church on a *union* basis, is to secure, as far as practicable, the harmonious cooperation of all those who love our Lord Jesus Christ, in one Church, without regard to past or present doctrinal views, or denominational differences. 2nd. That the Church, when organized, will be at liberty to select its pastor at will, from among all those evangelical ministers of whatever denomination, who have been commissioned by our Lord Jesus Christ to preach the everlasting gospel. 3d. It is further stated in By Law no. 4. that if any persons desire to exercise fellowship with the Church temporarily, without severing their connection with their own Church, they may be received into such fellowship, by presenting a certificate of good standing from their own churches.

4th. We desire, therefore, in view of these facts, that these principles and facts remain in full force, being satisfied with them, and believing that we can accomplish more for the Commissions we represent, and the Church universal in our present organization—as the work abundantly evidences—than if we are compelled to separate because of this unexpected and erroneous denominational character, set forth in the article alluded to above.

5th. We desire also to say that if this statement be allowed to go uncorrected, it will, we believe, not only impair a good begun work here, but will very much compromise, some of us, in the eyes of our own and other churches, and in the eyes of those persons in particular, with whom, and for whom we labor, and to whom we have continually held out the idea that *ours is an undenominational church*, free to all Christians of whatever name or order, race or color.

Hoping you may consider our statement favorably and give it as great publicity as the error it seeks to correct has had, we have the honor to be

Truly yours in Christian fellowship,
John Ogden, Prin. F.U.
Carrie M. Semple

Lidia [?] Lee	Mercilia E. White
	Hannah M. Swallow
Chas. Crosby	Ada Clapp
A. B. Ogden	Geo. L. White
	Laura C. White[124]

Ogden's statement was a little disingenuous since he had freely acknowledged to Cravath a few days earlier that "as I have often expressed to you and to others, I think I should prefer to see the Congregational Churches organized here, among others; but as I don't wish to change my church relations, and as I want to belong here, I much prefer our present plan [for a Union Church]." About the time that Ogden penned the lengthy exposition quoted above, a member of the Fisk staff, the Reverend H. S. Bennett, wrote—as a "back channel" to

---

[124] Ogden, *et al* to "Dear Brethren," 28 June 1868, AMA, Amistad.

Whipple in New York—that he had declined to sign the paper Ogden wrote, and went on to say that "the present position of the church at N[ashville]— i.e. Union and Independent—results from the fact that the Prof (Ogden) is a 'Methodist to the back bone.' "[125]

Although Rev. Strieby's response from New York to Ogden on behalf of the AMA officers seems to be missing from the archives, its thrust can be surmised from Ogden's next appeal.

Nashville, Tenn July 8th 1868

Rev. M.E. Strieby
    Secy. A.M.A. N.Y.
        Dear Br.

Yrs. of the 29th ult, to Br. Cravath, acknowledging the rect. of "the letters of Prof Ogden" was forwarded me this morning.

I wish to state in reply that it seems to me your treatment of said "plaster" is rather discourteous. In the first place, the communication is not a personal letter. It is not my communication any more than it is every person's whose name it bears, including every one of your teachers on the ground here who is a member of the church, and several others. I was urged to make this statement, in just the shape it is, so as to correct the error in the A[merican] M[issionary] and also to secure the publication of those of our Articles which were omitted (whether intentionally or not, I cannot tell) in the first published account of our organization.

Now I would not, personally, have any objection to your mode of correction, were it not for these facts. 1st. The teachers and friends whose statement said "plaster" is, have all left the South with the expectation that the correction will be made as we stated it. I therefor have no means of consulting them directly. 2nd. If it is left in the shape you propose, it does not settle the matter. It will not be six weeks before it will be claimed by parties here, as it has already been, to the detriment of our work, that our Church is a Congregational Church in everything but name, and that *that* will be added soon.

Now, my course may, at your distance appear a little captious. But Sir, *it is not*—and time will show it. If you were on the ground and knew all the circumstances, you would agree with me.

You may do as you think best about the publication of our "statement." But remember, I enter my individual protest against

---

[125] Ogden to Cravath, 20 June 1868; Bennett to Whipple, 20 June 1868; both AMA, Amistad.

its nonpublication.

Believing you have the good of our work at heart, I have the honor to be

                Yours truly John Ogden[126]

Ogden's final missive on this subject follows.

                Nashville, Tenn. July 20th 1868

Dear Br. Strieby,

         Yours of the 11th was recvd, just before starting to Cin[cinnati] where I have seen and conversed with Br. Cravath. I agree with you both, that for the mere correction of the verbal error, your statement is sufficient. But this is not the main thing. The "sore" was larger than you had any means of knowing; and it was for the purpose of preventing its' spreading that the "plaster" was prepared. Of course you knew nothing of this; hence you are entirely excusable for urging the nonpublication of our "statement." I could not explain this to you then without seeming to be in conflict with parties here [Bennett] with whom you are interested, and with whom we desire to live harmoniously, but who, unfortunately are not in full sympathy with our union movement as we understand it. It was to bring this matter to a definite understanding and settlement, that I was urged to prepare a statement and to insist upon its publication. Had that been done, it would have been a finality by mutual agreement; but as it now stands, we are liable to the same trouble again. But since the matter has assumed its present shape, we are willing to drop it, with this understanding. That if a similar trouble arises here, said "statement" or its equivalent must be published, as a matter of defense and safety.

You will find no warmer or truer friends of this Union Movement *as you understand and approve it,* than your present corps of teacher in this school. But when encroachments are made by parties not fully in harmony with it, and who express preferences for other arrangements and whose indiscretions are dangerous as well as annoying, then it becomes necessary, both for safety and success, to define the position so closely and clearly, that immediate and remote danger may be avoided. It was for these purposes, and *these alone*, and with the wish to implicate *no one*, that the statement was prepared. This matter would not even be

---

[126] Ogden to Strieby, 8 July 1868, AMA, Amistad.

alluded to now, were it not *necessary*, in order that you might fully comprehend the situation.

I ought to apologize, and do apologize to you for the indiscretion of making use of Mr. Cravath's letter from you, without first consulting him.

Hoping this explanation may be satisfactory, and with the highest regard I am,

Truly yours   John Ogden[127]

In many respects a union church was just the thing for Ogden personally and he felt it was for Nashville too for he thought it would help break down sectarianism. Moreover, the case Ogden made implicitly was one made many times in the Reconstruction period by Yankees working in the South: traditional white churches were too unemotional and did not appeal to Blacks. By moving to a union church solution the leaders might be able to slip into the service at least some aspects that might appeal to Blacks. Finally, the Blacks, and not just John and Gussie Ogden, would not have to leave whatever churches they already held membership in.

On the personal side—and note that Ogden's wife also signed the "Dear Brethren" letter—a union solution must have looked good. There can be no doubt, considering the innumerable mentions of religion and God in almost everything he wrote, that Ogden was a strong Christian believer. But it is also true that he was not much of a sectarian. It is not even clear what sect he inherited from his family. The evidence weighs most heavily for the Baptists, but it could have been the Methodists. As the AMA was Congregational, uninformed outsiders at times considered him a member of that faith. Eventually, following his wife, he became an Episcopalian. She herself was religiously mobile, having earlier switched from the Presbyterianism that she had inherited from her family in Wisconsin and Minnesota. John and Gussie Ogden's children were all baptized and confirmed in the Episcopal Church. But as we see further on, later in life Ogden participated actively with the Methodists at some moments.

One daughter reported that he took a light view of dogma and theological tenets and from her description he seems to have been almost

---

[127] Ogden to Strieby, 20 July 1868, AMA, Amistad. On this see also Richardson, *Christian Reconstruction*, 181-182; and Ogden to Whipple, 29 February 1868, and H.S. Bennett to Whipple, 20 June 1868, both AMA, Amistad.

anti-intellectual in his Christianity. She reports his speaking over the dinner table in a humorous commonsensical way about religion and quotes him as once saying, when apostolic succession was under discussion, that "I don't believe in the laying on of hands any more than in the laying on of feet!" This kind of levity—even if merely verbal—may not have helped him at Fisk.[128]

Towards blacks Ogden was usually sympathetic and he seemed to enjoy working with the Freedmen at Fisk, but at least once he commented skeptically and at length on their abilities and the amount of time it would take for them to overcome the inheritance of slavery. Even here though, the skepticism was modified by hope and an effort at kindness. E. P. Smith had apparently asked Ogden to forward examples of the remarkable abilities or performance of some of the students, and in reply Ogden urged caution and said that:

> I think that much harm has been done our cause by such whitewashed accounts. The fact is simply this: these people are not extraordinary in any of their peculiarities. I believe almost any race of people submitted to similar treatment and influences, would present similar characteristics both in vice and virtue. Few people who talk and write much about the Negro character seem to understand it. To say nothing about the susceptibility of this race of people, and their most unfavorable antecedents, it is a most lamentable fact that as a race they are exceeding low both in morals and intellect. And how could they be otherwise? They have endured enough to spoil an angelic nature. But the facts are here and the question is how to bring them out of this awful condition? My opinion is that one generation, at least, must pass away before we can look for much from these people.
> I never realized the deep and damning effects of human slavery until I was brought in close and daily contact with these people. Their depravity is frightful, and their ignorance mournful. Years and years and *years* of patient and persistent labor must ensue in order to remove these obstacles. Yet there is much, very much that is promising.

Ogden clearly was struggling here; on the one hand he did not want northerners to expect impossibilities from him at Fisk. He said that this

---

[128] Fragmentary letter, Mary Ogden Larimer to Dorene Heacock Larimer, undated [ca 1932] in Ogden Papers, author's possession.

kind of undue optimism "leads the people of the North to expect more than can be realized." Yet he believed strongly in education, was not a racist, and thus he inevitably thought that the Freedmen would progress even though considerable time might be required. His sentiments were to keep up the work. Still, the whole passage offers an uneasy kind of sympathy mixed with condescension and the repeated phrase, "these people," soon grated on black nerves.[129]

That was about as far in a negative direction as Ogden went; mostly he held benign views of blacks. In 1865 he had whimsically written that "[the Negro] is supposed to combine in himself and race all the evils of original sin, and a great many more added since the fall of humanity. The curse of Cain, the curse of Ham . . . and all the other curses down to John Tyler and James Buchanan are supposed to attach to him."[130]

More importantly, Ogden operated a racially integrated school (four or five white students usually appeared on the reports) and until the end of 1867 he persistently demanded racially unified schools. He began on this theme at the end of the war. In late 1865 concerning segregated schools Ogden asked rhetorically, "who. . .would think of providing two schools in a district, the one for the people of English origin and the other for Scotch; one for Germans, another for French; one for Chinese, another for Spaniards?" And he accurately predicted that if society were to give in and establish two separate school systems, "our work will all have to be done over again someday. . .and we shall pay dearly for our folly."[131]

For the next two years in Nashville Ogden pressed for racially integrated schools. In a controversial address before the Tennessee State Teachers' Association on 13 November 1867 he attacked the provision for segregated schools that the state legislature had enacted that year. One newspaper reported the speech as "Ogden's harangue" and Ogden's old

---

[129] Ogden to E.P. Smith, 8 May 1867, AMA, Amistad. Dan Carter did Ogden a grave injustice by citing this passage and placing it in a chapter entitled, "The Proslavery Argument in a World Without Slavery." See *When the War was Over*, 151.

[130] Ogden, in a letter published in the *New Era* (location unknown), 20 November 1865, quoted from a clipping scrapbook by Larimer, "Evaluation of Ogden," 146. The Library of Congress catalogue lists 180 newspapers named "New Era." I have not been able to identify which this was.

[131] Monthly School Reports, *passim*, 1867-1869, AMA, Amistad. Ogden, from the *New Era*, November 1865, quoted in Larimer, "Evaluation of Ogden," 147-148.

friend from Winona, Minnesota, Reverend Burt, following Ogden to the podium, called Ogden's views "radicalism," "visionary," and a "reckless innovation[.]" Even McKee disagreed with Ogden, although in comparatively measured terms. The Nashville *Republican Banner* ran the following detailed account of that afternoon's session, beginning with Ogden, and going through the responses of several other speakers:

Afternoon Session

The exercises were opened by singing. The President [Senator William Bosson] then announced that Professor John Ogden would deliver an address on the "relation which colored school bear to the educational system of the State," the address to be illustrated by exercises by the normal class of the Fisk University.

A class of fourteen scholars, half male and half female, was brought in front of the platform and examined. The exercises embraced, the most intricate problems in mental arithmetic. The examination was commenced by Mrs. Ogden, and continued by several of the scholars belonging to the class. The answers elicited were prompt, and almost invariably correct, reflecting great credit upon teachers and pupils.

After the class exercises were over Professor Ogden commenced his address. Schools, he said, formed one of the leading institutions of the country. The speaker here contrasted the North with the South, contending that in the late war, popular education was a source of strength to the former section, while a limited intelligence among the masses was a positive weakness to the South. Schools, common schools, are the levelers of caste, wealth, and distinction. They are intrinsically democratic, allowing no distinction between rich and poor, and if carried out to their legitimate end, not controlled by prejudice, would not make any discrimination on account of race or color. The common school system of Tennessee, considering the surroundings, is liberal and progressive, extending the privileges of education to both black and white, making distinctions between the races in minor particulars. As it is, the school system of our State approximates to perfection, but does not go far enough. In the school districts separate school are provided for the whites and blacks. This is wrong. It encourages caste and prejudice. Common school buildings should embrace both black and white indiscriminately, as one race is just as much entitled to the advantages of a popular education as the other. If the whites have any objection to going to a school where blacks are admitted, why, then, let them stay away. They ought not to be either coaxed or forced to attend, but justice and common sense should prevail, nevertheless. We must remove every obstacle from the path of progress. God intended no such distinctions as we recognize and legalize. Black and white children, if we would carry out the designs of Providence, must be treated exactly alike, showing no partiality whatever. These walls of prejudice which now unfortunately exist must fall sooner or later, and why not now commence the initiative in this much needed reform. Some of our school districts cannot afford two schools, and yet on account of a foolish prejudice, separate buildings must be provided to accommodate the blacks and whites. How long is this to last? It is unworthy of the age in which we live, and of the State of Tennessee. Be assured that the words white and black, as legal distinctions, and particularly as applied to our common schools, must for ever be abolished from our statute books. Principles are eternal, and there is nothing in the world more certain than that the great principle of the brotherhood of man, must be recognized and acted upon before we have reached the goal of right and human freedom. But the whole human family is sick, and the healing process must take place slowly before perfect health is secured. The popular heart beats hopefully, exhibiting evident signs of convalescence. In fifty, twenty, aye perhaps in ten years, color will make no distinction in out common brotherhood; black and white will kneel down together; they will received education from a common source, in the same school. Wait and see if the development of time does not bring this about. Christianity, the royal remedy, with healing in its wings, will attract humanity to a common standard, no matter what unjust laws may endeavor to effect in imposing class distinctions on account of race or color.

Rev. Mr. Burt made a rejoinder to Professor Ogden's harangue, but he said he had not prepared any address for the occasions, as he was not apprised by the Committee of Arrangements what particular subject he was to speak upon. As he was up, however, he would speak for a little time, but would be careful not to bring up the unpleasant and fiery reminiscences indulged in by the speaker which had preceded him. These he thought rather out of place in an educational Convention, as were some of the other jagged and impalatable remarks of the same speaker. He did not indorse the sort of radicalism embodied in the address of Professor Ogden, contending that it was visionary and impracticable. He believed in a practical radicalism, a system which could effect the most good without riding rough-shod over the sentiments and natural prejudices of the people. It is absolutely impracticable to bring the whites and blacks together in our common schools at the present time, and a wise expediency demands of us that we make the most of the school system we have got, without insisting on reckless innovations. Separate schools are desirable now, but those for colored scholars should be just as good, and have as efficient teachers as those provided for white scholars. Colored education however, must be recognized in the common school system of the State, and our legislators should afford all possible encouragement to the educational development of both white and black.

Rev. Mr. Robinson followed in a few remarks favoring separate schools, until the time should come, which was apparently far remote, when the races could be educated together. Let us take what we get with thankfulness, and not begin to pine for what is simply impracticable now.

Judge Mills being called upon, next addressed the Convention. He had witnessed school exhibitions without number in the North, but had never seen anything superior to the aptness of the colored scholars examined a little while ago. A prejudice which would debar a class exhibiting such marked traits of mental acumen from mixing with the whites in the common schools, was unworthy of the nineteenth century. Let us in our school systems have no distinction.

Mr. Brown, of Rutherford County, said he was quite convinced that the effort to hoist impracticable schemes upon our common school system, would sure defeat the system itself. The principle of mixing the races in common schools he thought was right enough, but it was quite impracticable to carry out such a plan now. Separate schools must be put up with for a time.

Rev. Mr. Hyden, of McMinn County, was the next speaker. He did not, he said, believe in expediency, but went for the right, regardless of consequences. Education without making any distinction of color was right, therefore he favored it.

Mr. Williams, member of the House of Representatives, remarked that he was a believer in expediency, and was quite satisfied that it was utterly impossible at the present to educate the races together.

Rev. Mr. McKee said that the popular sentiment was decidedly against mixed schools. The sentiment must be heeded for the present, otherwise there is nothing more certain than that you will defeat the system of popular education as it is now established. Proceed to force the system of mixed schools, and you will soon have the school buildings occupied by blacks alone. This theory of mixed education will not do just now.

Mr. Doughty, member of the House, declared himself for the most radical measures, letting expediency, as he said, go to the dogs. The Negro deserved to be admitted into all our common schools, and this right would be an outrage to withhold. We must recognize the colored folks as men and brothers, and not let a miserable prejudice keep asunder what God had joined together.

On motion, the Convention adjourned until 7 o'clock in the evening.[132]

Ogden's position was not popular among whites anywhere in the United States at that time and most scholars would probably agree that classroom racial integration was about the least likely form of racial contact that would have been tolerated in the South then.

Peabody Fund opposition to school integration began to tell on Ogden too. Dr. Sears, the Peabody Fund agent in the South, actually was in attendance at the Tennessee State Teachers' Annual Meeting, 13 and 14 November 1867, and he must have been horrified not only at Ogden's position, but at the forceful terms in which he stated it. Sears believed the only effective way to assist education in the South was by funding separate schools for white and black. As a matter of principle he allocated no funds to explicitly bi-racial schools. Yet, as noted above, within months of the time Ogden presented the above-quoted remarks Peabody money started coming to Fisk. We have no information on the interaction between Sears and Ogden and how this came to pass, but we can only assume that Sears forced Ogden to change his position--at least publicly--as a condition for receiving the money. Thus, with the overall societal pressure, and with the opposition of a Fund that was giving his school $800 per year, Ogden appears to have given up on classroom

---

[132] Article entitled, "Popular Education, Annual Meeting of the State Teachers' Association--First Day's Proceeding," Nashville *Republican Banner* 53:221 (14 November 1867). James Welch Patton, *Unionism and Reconstruction in Tennessee, 1860-1869* (Chapel Hill, 1934), 161-162, quoted a small part of the report of the same session from the Nashville *Daily Press and Times* (15 November 1867) but I have been unable to read the full original account from that newspaper because the sole repository that holds it for the date, the University of Tennessee Library at Knoxville, refuses to lend it, saying that it is out on long-term loan.

integration. In the end he appears to have fallen silent on this topic.[133]

During the era that Ogden worked in education the teaching of morality was heavily emphasized in schools; they were to produce not simply scholars but moral men. That view underlay almost everything that Ogden himself had written in his 1858 *Science of Education, and the Art of Teaching* and he held to it a decade later when he wrote concerning the alleged conflict between scientific and religious truth that "science and religion were made to go hand in hand" and that conversion to Christianity was the proper door into the kingdom of science as much as into the kingdom of heaven. The moral formation of students, seen as proceeding from a specifically Christian base, was thought to be as important, or more important, than building intellectual foundations. Ogden, along with nearly all serious thinkers at the time, thought that the two were inseparable.[134]

It followed, therefore, that what was considered Christian morality would be forcibly promoted, and that Fisk University would have strict rules for student conduct. Thus one young man by the name of Thomas Rutting fell afoul of the rules and was forced to write a confession—obviously demanded by the faculty—in which he admitted that "I have wrote to young ladies in the School . . . ." While the letter was directed to no one in particular, it was co-signed or witnessed by four staff—but not including John Ogden. It may be noted that Ogden and the faculty did not in these cases behave differently than parents demanded. Parents sometimes insisted that their children, girls especially, be closely watched, and other teachers from around Tennessee who were sending students to Fisk alerted Ogden that certain students might warrant close supervision.[135]

Ogden apparently had the Fisk students taught the existence of God utilizing the argument from design which he almost certainly got

---

[133] Foner, *Reconstruction*, 321-322; 366-367. Merle Curti, *The Social Ideas of American Educators* (New York, 1935), 263-264.

[134] Lucius Osgood, *Osgood's American Fifth Reader* (1872), cited in Ruth Miller Elson, "American Schoolbooks and 'Culture' in the Nineteenth Century," *Mississippi Valley Historical Review*, 46 (December 1959): 415-416. Ogden, in *American Missionary*, 13:10 (Oct 1869): 219. James Turner, *Without God, Without Creed: The Origins of unbelief in America* (Baltimore: Johns Hopkins University Press, 1985), shows the risks that Christian believers ran when they asserted that science and religion were consonant; see especially his summary of the point, 156-157.

[135] 5 March 1870 (H9503I), AMA, Amistad.

from William Paley's widely-used 1802 book, *Natural Theology: or, Evidences of the Existence and Attributes of the Deity Collected from the Appearances of Nature*.[136] Ogden used this book for informal classes in his 1864 prison camp; he knew it and had presumably used it before the war. Paley went through many editions and was very popular in schools and colleges; Ogden likely would have been taught it at Ohio Wesleyan, if not earlier.[137]

As with the male student who "had wrote" to a young lady, not all students at Fisk reveled in the heavy-handed Christian indoctrination. W.E.B. DuBois, probably the most prominent graduate Fisk University has ever had, and certainly the most impressive of the nineteenth-century alumni, later wrote that he was "affronted" by the textbook on "Christian Evidences" (probably Paley) that he was compelled to read at Fisk. He went on:

> At Fisk a very definite attempt was made to see that we did not lose or question our Christian orthodoxy. At first the effort seemed to me entirely superfluous, since I had never questioned my religious upbringing. Its theory had presented no particular difficulties: God ruled the world, Christ, and men did right, or tried to; otherwise they were rightly punished.

DuBois attended Fisk after Ogden had left, so he is not here speaking of Ogden specifically. Yet there is little doubt that the regime established by

---

[136] Paley's teleology as exposed in *Natural Theology* is today generally considered superficial and popular although well written and of overwhelming appeal in its time. Prolix, and not easily summarized, Paley saw "mechanisms, instrumentalities, or contrivances" in nature and he especially used the human body for examples—the bones and muscles that elaborately fitted together, for example, and the 'perfection' of the eye too, which was much utilized in his argument. From these he deduced that "there must have been an intelligence who designed and made the machine." Quotes from Elmer Sprague, "Paley," in *The Encyclopedia of Philosophy* (1967), s. v. For a deeper look that situates Paley within the realm of more profound philosophers and shows the unwarranted leaps he made, see William Fulton, "Teleology," in *The Encyclopedia of Religion and Ethics* (1910-1922), s.v.

[137] Ogden, "Adventures and Escapes," 19, WVM. Charles Darwin first thought Paley's argument "conclusive" but himself helped destroy it in his *The Origin of Species*; see W.W. Bartley, "What Was Wrong with Darwin?," *New York Review of Books*, 24:14 (15 Sept. 1977): 35. Ogden also mentioned Joseph Butler ("Adventures and Escapes," 13), whose *Analogy of Religion, Natural and Revealed, to the Constitution and Course of Nature* (1736) offered arguments Paley later developed. On design, see also Turner, *Without God. Without Creed*, 54-57, 96-97, 173, 178, 182, 187.

Ogden, keeping with the tenor of the times and Ogden's own opinions, was the one that DuBois criticized.[138]

During the five years John Ogden spent in Nashville, though he had little enough time for activities outside of work, family, and visits to his family in the North in summer, he carried on professional educational activities at least sporadically. First we have glimpses of his attempting to conduct teachers' institutes in Tennessee, secondly, he worked in Nashville and in Tennessee to build support for public schools, third, he tried to organize the teachers of Tennessee into a state-wide body in order to further their interests and that of education in the state, and finally, he served in national education organizations, becoming national president of one section of the National Education Association by 1870.

The only teachers' institutes that appear in the record came in the 1868-1869 school year. They fell under the aegis of the Freedmen's Bureau Education agent (the successor of Ogden and Burt), and Ogden did not organize them, but was invited to participate. We cannot tell if they were for black teachers, white teachers, or both. One at Shelbyville, about fifty miles south of Nashville, did not go well in January 1869 and had to be cut off after only four of the scheduled six days. The following month Ogden did successfully conduct an institute in Knoxville, but we have no details.[139]

Ogden was interested, as noted earlier, in the state of public schools and their funding in Tennessee. Once the public school law was passed he continued to encourage classroom integration, probably not only for the obvious reasons he gave—financial and administrative practicalities— but because he believed that such conditions might provide openings for black teachers and thus jobs for his Fisk graduates. In retrospect the thought of black teachers in white or mixed classrooms at that time sounds utopian, but Ogden seems still to have envisioned it in 1868 when

---

[138] *The Autobiography of W. E. B. DuBois* (New York, 1968), 127. See also McPherson, *Abolitionist Legacy*, 198, n. 33. Overall DuBois had a favorable view of his years at Fisk. He said that Erastus Cravath, president when he was there, was "honest and sincere." See DuBois, *Dusk of Dawn: An Essay Toward an Autobiography of a Race Concept* (New York, 1940), 30-31, in McPherson, "White Liberals and Black Power in Negro Education, 1865-1915," *American Historical Review* 75 (June 1970): 1358, n. 3.

[139] Henry L. Swint, "Notes and Comments: Reports from Educational Agents of the Freedmen's Bureau in Tennessee, 1865-1870," THQ 1 (March-December 1942): 65. Ogden to Smith, 15 February 1869, AMA, Amistad.

he mentioned the idea in the following letter to Whipple in New York, obviously intending it for publication in the *American Missionary* as an informal report on the good work being done in the South.

        Nashville, Tenn. Feb. 29, 1868

Rev. Geo. Whipple
Dear Sir:

 Yrs. of the 26th is recvd. In conformity with your request allow me to say that brief sketches of the history of our institution have been published from time to time; and that I shall only speak, very briefly now, of its present plans and prospects.

Normal Classes

We have more than realized our most sanguine expectations since the incorporation of our school as per above "heading". Its most distinctive characteristic has been, from the beginning, a normal or training school for colored teachers, though some white children have availed themselves of the advantages of the school; among these one young man, a German by birth, who is now teaching with marked success.

 The first normal class of 12 was organized in November 1867. All are still members of the school, and are doing as well, or better, I think, than any class of equal attainments, I ever had, and I have had many. A second class of ten was organized in Jan. who are doing nearly as well. These two form two sections from which permanent details are made for teaching in the Model school (as per enclosed "Declarations" [not found]).The Model School is composed of about 60 pupils ranging in age from four to 14 and in advancement, from 0 to the 4th reader, primary arithmetic, and geography. This school is taught mainly by the 1st Division of Normal pupils. Two classes are in operation all the time of teaching, a recitation room being attached. This is the grand characteristic of the school at present, and does more to make good thorough teachers, than a half doz. academies and colleges. I meet one section of the teacher's class daily in my recitation room, where I give them a sound drill both in theory and practice together with a review of their course of studies from day to day.

 During Dr. Sears' visit South he spent the most of one day examining the school and the workings of my plans. Since then he has sent me $800 to be expended upon 16 of the most promising teachers I can select from the materials in the state, during the present year, on conditions similar to those named in "Declarations." I am now gathering these from all parts of the state. This class will and must be the crowning excellence of our school; and an inducement for future and larger donations from the Peabody fund—and other sources.

We have purchased apparatus worth about $350, and are making a beginning in that direction of study. A class of 12 or 15 has been formed in Latin, and other branches are receiving like attention.

The rebels look upon us with jealous eyes, and still aver that the "*Niggers*" "Can't learn." But it is not beyond even the probabilities, in my opinion, that *their children*, if taught at all, will be taught by colored teachers before ten years.

The religious interest among our pupils is most excellent and promising. Some 12 or 15 have been converted within the last week or two and the work is still increasing. A union church will be organized in a short time on the broad and Catholic basis of "Universal Brotherhood," Dr. Boynton to the contrary notwithstanding. Nearly every pupil in the school, of responsible age, is now either a professor of religion, or seeking it. May the good work go on!

Our school numbers now about 200, about one half adults. Our average and order are good, much better than at first. A literary society has been organized by the young men, and promises to be a success and a power.

To conclude allow me to say, that if this school, with its present advantages, can only be managed, so as to run it clear of any ecclesiastical complications, [it] can be made the leading State Normal University in the state of Tenna.

I hope the friends North will have the good sense to see this, for nothing is so much needed now, to aid the colored people and aid the white people and *all*, as thorough, well trained Christian teachers.

               Truly yours John Ogden

                               Prest.[140]

In any case, Ogden, leader of an institution that not only trained teachers but taught hundreds of children in lower-level classes each year, had gone before the Nashville Board of Education the year before, in 1867, to propose cooperation, apparently offering to take students that the Board of Education could not accommodate. His proposal was rejected, the

---

[140] Ogden to Whipple, 29 February 1868, AMA, Amistad. I have not identified "Dr. Boynton."

Board replying that it was able to handle all those who sought to enroll.[141]

While still working for General Fisk Ogden had tried to organize a teachers' convention for the summer of 1866 but was unable to do so. The following year he suggested one at Chattanooga, but the people there feared that such a meeting might cause trouble because of local prejudice so it appears that the convention was moved to Nashville for November 1867.[142] Toward the end of his time in Tennessee, Ogden also gave attention to national education organizations. The year before he left Nashville, after some indecisiveness, he went to Trenton, New Jersey, for the annual conference of the National Education Association. He was or became the first vice president of its Normal School Division and that led to his becoming its president the following year.[143]

Thus, the summer he moved from Nashville to take the position of "Principal of the Preparatory Department" of Kenyon College in Gambier, Ohio, he served as president of the Normal School Division of the National Education Association. Ogden presided at the annual meeting held 15 August 1870 at Central High School in Cleveland, and offered the presidential address.[144]

---

[141] Nashville Board of Education to Ogden, 30 August 1867, AMA, Amistad. On a slightly different aspect of these issues, see Howard N. Rabinowitz, "Half a Loaf: The Shift from White to Black Teachers in the Negro Schools of the Urban South, 1865-1900," *Journal of Southern History*, 40:4 (November 1974): 572.

[142] Edward F. Williams to Ogden, 17 April 1866; letter H 9204a, 8 March 1867, both AMA, Amistad.

[143] Ogden to Strieby, 25 June and 12 July 1869, AMA, Amistad.

[144] Larimer, "Evaluation of Ogden," 13, 74.

CHAPTER 6
Leaving Nashville, 1870

That August day in 1870 in Cleveland was the high point of John Ogden's career in education. Afterward he did not stop trooping: he directed four more normal schools and was elected Superintendent of Public Instruction in one western state, but these were the conventional jobs of a conventional educator. They were unlike his ground-breaking years at Fisk. When he left Fisk in the summer of 1870 and took his bows in Cleveland before the National Education Association, he stepped off the stage of history. Although John Ogden almost certainly did not know that he was leaving the limelight—and hardly recognized that he had been in it in the first place—his departure from Fisk was a move from the heroic to the pedestrian.

Why did John Ogden leave Fisk in 1870? There are as many answers as scholars who have casually considered it. Taking the Freedmen's Bureau job and the Fisk leadership position together, Ogden had spent five years at Nashville; that was not a short time in that environment, especially since he preceded it with several years of war in the same inhospitable region. His successor, Adam Spence, also stayed for five years, a stretch that some scholars have considered longer than average. Joe Richardson, for example, stated that "most of the teachers were northerners who considered themselves missionaries. Occasionally their commitment was long-term, but more often it was one to three years."[145]

Other evaluators have concluded that the Fisk faculty did not like Ogden, and especially that they did not care for Mrs. Ogden. The way the school was organized toward 1870, the three top men were Ogden, H.S. Bennett, and George L. White, followed in order by their three wives. This was the way the *American Missionary* listed the Fisk staff for the academic year 1869-1870:

Prof. John Ogden	Nashville, Tenn.
Rev. H. S. Bennett	Nashville, Tenn.
Mr. Geo. L. White	Nashville, Tenn.
Mrs. John Ogden	Nashville, Tenn.

---

[145] Richardson, *Christian Reconstruction*, 135-136.

Mrs. H. S. Bennett	Nashville, Tenn.
Mrs. Geo. L. White	Nashville, Tenn.
Miss Carrie Semple	Cincinnati, O.
Miss Sarah L. Hayden	Bedford, O.
Mrs. M. J. Robinson	Edgefield, Tenn.
Miss Helen C. Morgan	Oberlin, O.
Miss Julia A. Maginness	Colamer, O.
Miss L. Mina Stratton	Unionville, O.
Miss Julia E. Benedict	Woodbury, Conn.
Miss E. W. Douglass	Decorah, Iowa
Miss Addie Appleby	Oberlin, O.
Mrs. L. E. Aray	Nashville, Tenn.
Miss Ella Sheppard	Cincinnati, O.
Miss L. A. Cowan	Crawfordsville, Ind.

By this time Mrs. Ogden was serving as matron of the boarding department without pay, and that position cannot have been an easy one because of the lack of resources; in any event, there is no evidence that she possessed a lovable personality. Near the end of Ogden's time in Nashville, George White said that Ogden, and especially Mrs. Ogden, would have to go. But only four months earlier he had said that Ogden was indispensable to the development of the university. Thus the evidence is mixed on faculty comity. We will return to this subject.[146]

There were also minor conflicts between the Nashville contingent and the American Missionary Association headquarters in New York. In 1869 Secretary Whipple complained to Ogden that the AMA had not been given mention in a certain Fisk school circular; a few weeks later E.P. Smith registered a complaint of the same type—that some sort of "notice" had gone out that did not mention the AMA. Ogden replied that he considered their support so intrinsic that it was hardly thought of, but that in future he would be glad to insert whatever notice in circulars that Smith thought desirable. He went on: "But let me say to you and to all our friends and helpers, that this way of insinuating and finding fault with our work, is the surest way to discourage us, and impede the progress of our work." A month earlier Ogden had specifically asked Strieby for encouragement, saying "write to us occasionally. We feel weak

---

[146] The list for the academic year 1869-1870 carries the heading, "Commissioned at Cincinnati and supported by the Western Freedmen's Aid Commission and the A.M.A." *American Missionary*, 14:6 (June 1870): 125; Taylor, "Fisk University," unpub. MS, 73.

and weary betimes; and a word from a man whose heart is warm on all sides does us good." Clearly there were moments after four years when Ogden did not feel appreciated by the New York office. And if he had felt any closer to the WFAC influence in the Cincinnati joint AMA/WFAC office, he soon lost that contact too, for in March 1870 the Western Freedmen's Aid Commission disappeared altogether, merged into the AMA.[147]

Earlier we noted the disagreement over mission at Fisk: would it be a normal school or a university? Beyond that, little that was new came up towards the end of Ogden's Nashville years. But A.A. Taylor, looking back on 1870 from evidence accumulated years later, mentioned as important in Ogden's decision the fact that both the board *and faculty* had voted to set Fisk up as a university and to establish university courses; that could have made Ogden feel an outsider. College courses were first offered only in 1871 after Ogden left, with the first class of five graduating in 1875. We do not know exactly what Ogden felt about the university matter; did he feel insecure? He had once commented to Barnard that he had no classical education but that he doubted that Latin was needed in Minnesota. Did he still feel that way about Fisk and Tennessee in 1870? Did he just not want to get involved with university administration when he felt comfortable with normal school work? Was he miffed that the board and faculty had outvoted him? We do not know. But commentators of the period felt strongly that normal school functions and university functions could not well coexist.[148]

"Family" is one of the most conventional reasons offered when resigning a job. Because it is so common it is often not fully believed. Upon Ogden's resignation from Fisk such reasons were not absent: "At the close of the year [1869-1870] Professor Ogden tendered his resignation as principal, the circumstances of his family seeming to demand a change." In this case, however, the family may have been more than a trite excuse. Ogden and his wife had two children, John Junior and

---

[147] Ogden to Smith, 18 June 1869; Ogden to Strieby, 4 May 1869, AMA, Amistad; *American Missionary*, 14:5 (May 1870): 112. The disappearance of the WFAC may have been a formality. As early as 1867 their joint WFAC/AMA Cincinnati-office letterhead made them look like one organization. See Cravath to N. E. Whiting, 14 November 1867, AMA, Amistad.

[148] Taylor, "Fisk University," unpub. MS, 73; Ogden to Barnard, 31 December 1859, Barnard Papers, New York University; Curry, *History of the Peabody Education Fund*, 121.

Arthur, both born in Nashville. Larimer reported that they wanted to rear their children in the North which they considered a better and safer place for them—a not unreasonable assumption.

Furthermore, Mrs. Ogden had career interests—or soon developed them—and that may have influenced her to want to leave her unpaid Fisk job as kitchen matron. Three years after arriving in Ohio, thinking in terms of the education of her small children, she interested herself in the kindergarten movement, traveled to Boston, and received training in the Froebel method from Mary J. Garland and Elizabeth P. Peabody. Returning to Ohio she established kindergartens in Cleveland and Columbus. Anna Brewster Ogden remained active in the kindergarten movement the rest of her life.[149]

The last family consideration that may have motivated the Ogdens' departure was simply money and benefits. Earlier in the development of education in the United States a semi-altruistic devotion to teaching had predominated. By the late 1860s, however, partly under the "professionalization" pressure, educators began to think of teaching as more than a psychological stance, more than a mere service activity. They felt that adequate compensation based upon longevity, disability retirement when warranted, and life insurance were deserved benefits for practitioners in what they considered a significant profession. In 1870, Ogden, with a wife and two small children, may have reflected on the more than twenty-five years he had spent in the profession and contrasted that with his modest salary, and the absence of any security.[150]

Moreover, in 1869 and 1870 evidence was accumulating that Northern eleemosynary support for the freedmen's aid societies was diminishing; no one could know then that the drop was not going to be permanent, and that after a decade or two financial support would pick up again. In 1869, however, contributions to the AMA began to drop and did not rise to the 1869 level again until 1888. The situation was similar with the aid societies collectively except that their overall income peak came a year later—in 1870—and they worked their way back up to that

---

[149] Ogden Pension Record, 10 January 1899, NA. Larimer, "Evaluation of Ogden," 8; she probably based this statement upon family lore and tradition to which she had access. *Ohio State Journal*, 31 March 1901, cited in Larimer, 8. Ogden to Cravath, 11 January 1873 and 23 July 1873, AMA, Amistad.

[150] *Special Report of the [National] Commissioner of Education* [Barnard], 249, 253, cited in MacMullen, *Henry Barnard*, 274. Bledstein, *Culture of Professionalism*, has little on this aspect of professionalism in higher education.

level in 1881. At Fisk University the physical condition of the wooden barracks was not improving with time and it was evident by 1870 or 1871 that the school would soon face major fundraising, a probable relocation, and a new building campaign. No one then at Fisk could foresee that a group called the Jubilee Singers were going to issue forth from the school the very next year and bring in the money needed for the move, and the new building. Thus when John Ogden resigned in 1870 to go North the financial future and physical plant picture at Fisk looked worse than at any time since its opening in January 1866.[151]

In addition, the earlier-vaunted enthusiasm of the Freedpeople for education was being tested around 1868-1870. It had often been said during and just after the Civil War that when liberation came to the slaves their pent-up desire for education and literacy pushed tens and hundreds of thousands of them into classrooms where they aspired to learn to read. It is clear that at that early time the Freedmen did not understand that education is not an either/or matter—either you have it or you don't. They believed that the process of becoming literate was a straightforward task that could be mastered in a relatively brief time, and when they had attained literacy they would be "educated." A little later, when they began to grasp that education was a gradual process that offered only incremental gains and required a lot of time, favorable circumstances, suitable teachers, and physical facilities, many became discouraged. After three years the newly-freed grasped the enormity of the catch-up job they faced. This disheartening realization sent many to the educational sidelines.[152]

---

[151] McPherson, *Abolitionist Legacy*, Fig. 2, p. 147. Ronald E. Butchart, "Educating for Freedom: Northern Whites and the Origins of Black Education in the South, 1862-1875," Ph.D. diss., SUNY-Binghamton, 1976, graph, p. 493 has slightly different figures. Hopkins, *Life of Fisk*, 112-113.

[152] Edward S. Philbrick, writing from the Sea Islands on 21 November 1865, after three years of experience, concluded much the same thing about *both* the ex-slaves and the benevolent societies. "It will take many years to make an economical and thrifty man out of a freedman, and about as long to make a sensible and just employer out of a former slaveholder. It is not at all likely that the Southern community will tax itself to educate the Negro yet for a good while, and I have my doubts whether the system of education thus far carried on through the benevolence of Northern and English communities can be kept up much longer. It is a laudable and a noble work, but I fear it can't be sustained after the novelty is over. There seems to be a lethargy creeping over our community on this subject, which is very hard to shake off. The feeling is somewhat general that the Negro must make the most of his chances and pick up his a, b, c's as he can. Moreover,

Leaving Nashville

A teacher's letter published in the AMA magazine the year Ogden resigned listed eight impediments to black progress in the South. The teacher had some years of experience in the South and could even have been Ogden himself since some of the views expressed were similar to those we know he held. The impediments listed were:

1. Lack of role models in learned professions or business.
2. Inadequate idea of what education is—i.e., only the three Rs.
3. Lack of educated influence in the home; will require a century to change.
4. "Natural stupor," i.e., hereditary shortcomings. (In an unconscious contradiction the teacher said that these hereditary shortcomings could be overcome by a pure home, religion, and literature, i.e., by environment, the opposite of heredity.)
5. Servile and deceitful habits.
6. Want of character.
7. Misled by ignorant leaders, generally preachers.
8. Violence by their enemies.

The last we will return to below; numbers 4-6 fall into a class discussed earlier. Number 7 may well be true, but it is difficult to interpret without more detail. However, the first three were undoubtedly accurate observations and reflected circumstances that could not only retard "progress" generally, but profoundly affected the Freedman's attitude toward, and aptitude for, education. Almost everyone became aware of these three problems about the time Ogden left Fisk.[153]

In Tennessee discouragement was not limited to blacks and to John Ogden. John Alvord, the Washington-based General Superintendent of Schools for the Freedmen's Bureau, said that with the 1869 change in the

---

there is a mass of ignorance in the South under *white* skins, which is likely to give us more immediate trouble, politically, than the ignorance of the Negro, for that latter is not as yet armed with the suffrage. Of course there is not much enthusiasm about sending teachers South to teach the poor whites, so the Negro suffers from the magnitude of the undertaking, from his remoteness from view, and the general disposition among mankind to let everybody hoe their own weeds so long as they don't shade one's own garden." Elizabeth W. Pearson, ed., *Letters from Port Royal Written at the Time of the Civil War* (New York, 1969;first pub. 1906), 317-318.

[153] *American Missionary*, 14:12 (December 1870): 281-282; Swint and Butchart, while sharing little else, agree on this. See Henry L. Swint, *Northern Teacher in the South, 1862-1870* (Nashville, 1941), 74, and Butchart, *Northern Schools, Southern Blacks*, 98-114.

Tennessee public school law withdrawing public support from schools for Freedmen, the news from Tennessee was generally dispirited. From Tennessee he reported decreasing numbers of schools, discouragement on the part of local supporters, diminution of operations of the benevolent societies, loss of students, and loss of teachers. "The general tone of all correspondence from Tennessee is despondent, betraying much anxiety for the future . . . . [but] . . . the benevolent societies are, with great effort, still maintaining high and normal schools in the large towns and cities." Alvord himself resigned in the fall of 1870 because the Freedmen's Bureau was being snuffed out.[154]

The final possible factor leading to Ogden's departure from Nashville was the resistance of the whites to schooling for Negroes. There was, of course, no unified caucasian position on the matter; some whites during some periods believed that education would be beneficial to blacks in ways that would also prove useful to the dominant group. Other whites were indifferent. Neither of these groups posed problems for Ogden and other northern educators. White attitudes, however, varied during Ogden's five years in Tennessee, and during some periods sub-stantial numbers of intransigent white Tennesseans were violently hostile to Freedmen's education and therefore dangerous to blacks and to Northern schoolteachers. Henry L. Swint, a Tennessee historian writing during an earlier period of Reconstruction interpretation (the 1930s), summarized the phases this way.

> There is ample evidence to support the conclusion that the Southern people were not united in complete opposition to the education of the Negro. On the contrary, there was very little opposition until 1867, and it was not until 1868 that violence became prevalent throughout the South. After the election of 1868 this spirit of opposition declined, until by 1870, there was little outward manifestation of opposition.[155]

The tenor of Swint's book was that Southerners opposed northern whites teaching blacks because they feared it would be effective in leading blacks to reach for social equality. He said:

---

[154] J.W. Alvord, General Superintendent, Schools, Bureau of Refugees, Freedmen and Abandoned Lands; *Tenth Semi-Annual Report on Schools for Freedmen*; 1 July 1870. Washington, 1870; Butchart, *Northern Schools, Southern Blacks*, 100.

[155] Swint, *Northern Teacher in the South*, 132-133.

> The Southern reaction to the presence of the Yankee teacher was definite, decided, and violent. At first the teachers were tolerated, but as they increased in numbers and influence, the Southern people saw their worst fears realized. The teachers associated with the Negro on terms of social equality, some of them even going to far as to avoid all contact with white people, devoting themselves exclusively to the society of the Negro. They urged the Negro to assert his individuality, to demand that his former master speak to him by "title" instead of by given name.... The Southerner did not fear the education of the Negro—he feared Negro education in the hands of the typical "Yankee teacher," under the program of education advanced by the radical legislatures.[156]

Whites thought that education by northern teachers might lead southern blacks to be less malleable than before liberation. In general, the southern brouhaha that Swint described proves that Southern whites believed—indeed feared—that education would do something for blacks. Some Southerners claimed that blacks could not learn, but they obviously feared that the former slaves would learn too well and would seek some kind of equality.

Contrasting with Swint's depiction of white resistance in Tennessee as sometimes moderate, recent scholars have portrayed Tennessee as an almost uniquely evil, reactionarily innovative state of crude and brutal whites. They point out that Tennessee hatched the Klan in 1866, introduced a discriminatory poll tax in 1870 and was the first state to legalize segregation—in 1881. Thus the Klan which started in 1866 became politically significant in 1867 and began a campaign to put the state back into the hands of the Democrats, a goal attained in 1870. While there were ups and downs in Klan efforts, it would not have been unreasonable for Ogden to fear that their successes up to 1870 were going to lead to yet worse conditions.[157]

Some scholars have asserted that Klan activity and violence affected attendance at Fisk in 1869. Ogden admitted in October of that year that attendance had been down the preceding academic year, but asserted that when the students who were out teaching came back around Christmastime total attendance would rise to about 300. Eighteen sixty-nine was the

---

[156] Swint, *Northern Teacher in the South*, 94-95.

[157] William Gillette, *Retreat from Reconstruction, 1869-1879* (Baton Rouge: Louisiana State University Press, 1979), 41, 28.

year that the Tennessee legislature repealed the state education law, effectively ending public education for blacks in all of Tennessee except Nashville and Memphis. While this would not have affected Ogden directly, he might have experienced it as a discouragement inasmuch as it would tend to reduce the demand for his black normal school graduates.[158]

Perhaps it was Nashville, or Ogden's easy and unthreatening personality, but only one reported instance of physical unpleasantness or threat to Ogden is known, and it was mild indeed compared to the murders, beatings, burnings and other offenses recorded elsewhere throughout Tennessee and the South. According to the story that came down through the family, he and the family were in their apartment in one of the Fisk barracks buildings one night when masked figures came up to their quarters, but finding the building in darkness went away. Ogden and his wife were in the darkened rooms looking out.[159]

No matter how one looks at Ogden's five years in Tennessee black education—whether one considers Andrew Johnson, general white resistance, the rise of the Ku Klux Klan, the "Redemption" of Tennessee, or the failure of the state to found and maintain public education for blacks—Ogden was working in a hostile and wearying environment. One Southerner, a Maryland judge who presided over some of the Klan trials in the South expressed it well in a private letter to his wife. About the KKK people he said that he never knew that "the beast was so close under the skin of men." That phrase captures well the psychology and behavior of altogether too many white people in Tennessee during Ogden's years there.[160]

The above recapitulates the many reasons John Ogden and his wife might have had to leave Fisk and Nashville and go back North. After this litany, one can readily imagine their concluding that they could live better, safer, and in a more civilized way back in Ohio, *and* give their children sound educational opportunities.

The matter was not entirely one-sided, however. There were pulls

---

[158] Richardson, *Christian Reconstruction*, 137; Ogden to E.P. Smith, 18 October 1869, AMA, Amistad; Foner, *Reconstruction*, 422.

[159] Larimer, "Evaluation of Ogden," 7.

[160] Foner, *Reconstruction*, 178-183; Hugh L. Bond to Anna Bond, 20 September 1871, in Bond Papers, Maryland Historical Society, quoted in Gillette, *Retreat from Reconstruction*, 28.

to remain. In 1869 Dr. Barnabas Sears reported that he found Fisk "the best normal school he had seen in the South" and recommended giving money there rather than to Berea. Ogden had other friends too in places where it counted. E.P. Smith recognized—a few years later when it did not help much—"Some of you know [the early days] by heart. I wish your President [Cravath] and his wife and Prof. Ogden were with you today. What it cost then and costs now to be identified with and responsible for such a school, none of us who have not tried it can know." Even one of the local papers found something good to say about Ogden—again when it was too late to make a difference: "We much regretted the departure of Prof. Ogden some months since, but are satisfied that the conduct of the institution under Prof. Spence is entirely satisfactory."[161]

In spite of the rumors that Ogden and wife were not well liked by the Fisk faculty, for two or three years after their departure there were a number of expressions of friendliness back and forth between the Ogdens and the faculty who remained in Nashville. After Ogden left Fisk on 1 August 1870, and made the stop in Cleveland for the N.E.A. meeting, he went to Gambier, Ohio, to become principal of the preparatory department of Kenyon College. At the end of the month he wrote George White and promised to forward some money for a note on some "lots." It appears that he had bought lots in Nashville, apparently expecting to remain longer than he did. He was short on cash as he moved to Ohio and said so explicitly; he would not likely have committed himself to property payments in Nashville if he had foreseen that he was soon to leave. In closing the letter to White Ogden expressed sympathy for the illness of White's son and reported that his own "little ones are well. All send much love."[162]

A few weeks later he wrote further to White, talked about the health of their children, and graciously said, "permit me to congratulate you on your good fortune in securing Prof. Spence. I think he is just the man. The F[isk] U[niversity] should now arise—and it will. God speed you all in the good work." He added that "you and Laura must make

---

[161] Source uncertain, perhaps *Peabody Proceedings*, Vol. 1 or 2, quoted in Horace Mann Bond, *The Education of the Negro in the American Social Order* (New York, 1934), 131; "Remarks of E.P. Smith at Services of Dedication", 40; *Tennessee Republican*, quoted in *American Missionary*, 15:5 (May 1871): 113.

[162] Ogden to White, about 26 August 1870, AMA, Amistad.

your calculations to come and see us next summer and spend a month with us."[163]

The correspondence with White continued into the next year and there Ogden revealed more about the psychological state he had been in in 1870.

> Now George, stick to it as long as you can stand it; when you get clear worn out, and are good for nothing at all, quit, come North and see me. Brush around among folks a little and you will get well. I did. 'You are doing a glorious work,' as they used to tell me, but telling one a thing that he knows, or even that he don't know, don't ease his burdens much.[164]

At commencement time in 1871 he added:

> It is impossible for me to tell how deeply I regret my inability to be with you this week. All the cherished memories of the past at Nashville, all the bright hopes for the future of F[isk] U[niversity] made real by the light of the living realities of the present urge me to go.... But tell the Board, tell the teachers, tell the *School* my heart is there; my prayers go up daily for their prosperity, and my chief concern is now, as when with you in the body, how to give the largest and best opportunities to the people, *all* the people, for a thorough education of heart, head, and body.
> ...
> Please remember me to all the Board, but especially to E. M. [Cravath] and to that large hearted man—Gen. Fisk—if he is present. And tell him I have not left the field. I am only taking breath for a more vigorous effort.[165]

In October 1871, after the Ogdens had moved on to Worthington, Ohio, where he became co-proprietor of the Ohio Central Normal School, they had occasion to host the later-famous Fisk Jubilee Singers who were then traveling into the North on their first tour of concerts to raise money for Fisk University. The Jubilee Singers had traveled through eight Ohio cities and towns and, arriving "at Worthington, they met a

---

[163] Ogden to White, 13 and 17 September 1870, AMA, Amistad.

[164] Ogden to White, 28 April 1871, AMA, Amistad.

[165] Ogden to White, 19 June 1871, AMA, Amistad.

hearty welcome from Professor Ogden and his wife, their old instructors at Fisk, who had done work of lasting value in laying its foundations, but were now in charge of the Ohio State [sic] Normal School at that place. There they remained for several days for much-needed rest, giving a concert meanwhile which, thanks specially to the activity of these two old friends, yielded $60."[166]

These fragments of evidence are not unambiguous, but the Ogdens clearly left an impression at Fisk, though they were perhaps better loved after their departure than when on the scene. But it is clear that they were tired and worried when they suddenly left in 1870, and they hoped to find in Ohio a less stressful situation. They did not elicit fervent affection from their colleagues. Perhaps Joe Richardson summed up Ogden in Nashville as accurately as anyone: Ogden had done well at Fisk. He was not particularly well-liked by white people, but they respected his ability and sincerity.[167]

---

[166] J.B.T. Marsh, *The Story of the Jubilee Singers* (Boston, 1880), 20; Richardson, "Fisk University," THQ 29:1 (1970): 39.

[167] Richardson, *Ibid.*

CHAPTER 7
Some Good Years, Some Bleak Years: Work in Ohio, Washington, D.C., and North Dakota

In the fall of 1870 Ogden started with the new venture at Kenyon College, but he lasted only one academic year. His department in Milnor Hall (a half-mile from the main campus) was called the Kenyon Grammar School, and had been known as the preparatory school of Kenyon College. The 1870-1871 catalogue stated that instruction would be given for students desiring to prepare for the teaching profession, thus Ogden was able to preserve a normal-school teaching function for himself. On the whole, however, it is impossible to believe that he or his wife considered the Kenyon situation as a rise in position. That realization only increases the uncertainty that one feels in trying to account for their departure from Nashville. Did they have to leave quickly? Could they not take the time to locate something more suitable?[168]

Milnor Hall was organized as an entrepreneurial adjunct to Kenyon College. In effect, Ogden had a contract, served as principal, and Mrs. Ogden ran the boarding and lodging facilities. Such an arrangement was common. But toward the end of the academic year, in the spring of 1871, Ogden wrote White, "but George, this is my last term here. I have just made arrangements to go into a Normal School enterprise in Central Ohio, near Columbus .... Mr. Wm. Mitchell, Supt. of Pub. Inst. at Columbus for the last 6 years, and myself have purchased the property, and we expect to open the affair in the fall. I think it is just what I want .... It is a beautiful place, and we have every prospect of making it a grand thing."[169]

Knowing the shortness of his tenure at Milnor Hall seemed to have led Ogden to describe it unflatteringly. At the end of his stay there he described Milnor Hall as "a little 7 by 9 concern, not worth the great toe of Fisk University." Ogden stated clearly from Ohio on more than one

---

[168] "Catalogue of Kenyon College, and of the Theological Seminary, of the Diocese of Ohio, For the year 1870-1871, Gambier" (Columbus, 1871), esp. pp. 26-28, "Kenyon Grammar School." Ms. Jami Peelle, Special Collections Librarian, Kenyon College, kindly provided copies.

[169] Ogden to White, 28 April 1871, AMA, Amistad.

occasion what he thought the promise and importance of Fisk University was, the affection which he held for those associated with it, and how at Gambier he felt left on a shelf. He closed this letter by asking to be remembered to the Fisk University Board. Ogden did not see Milnor Hall as acceptable, and hoped for a larger success at Worthington where he was to remain for ten years, until 1881.[170]

For one year Ogden shared the ownership and management of the Ohio Central Normal School (housed in a structure that had formerly been a female seminary) with William Mitchell; they were listed as Associate Principals, with Mitchell getting the top listing. In 1872 M. H. Lewis replaced Mitchell as the Associate Principal with John Ogden. Lewis withdrew in January, 1875 and Ogden was henceforth the only Principal and the sole proprietor. By 1877 the institution became the "Ohio Central Normal and Kindergarten Training School, " with Mrs. Ogden listed as the "Kindergartner." In this environment Ogden was largely occupied with his beloved teacher-training and with general administration. After the stress of Nashville it must have been comforting to remain in the pleasant almost-suburb of Columbus, directing his school and doing normal-school training.[171]

During the last years of the 1870s at the Ohio Central Normal School Ogden returned to scholarly and professional writing. He had always written prolifically both in prose and poetry. Besides the textbooks and other professional writing done before the Civil War he also kept the poetry journal during the war, and in later years he accumulated many pages of manuscripts that are still among his papers, unpublished. As administrator of Fisk and the man who had the responsibility to report to the entire interested national community on its work, he had been incessantly occupied writing letters, articles, and reports. As co-manager and then chief of the normal school at

---

[170] Ogden to White, 19 June 1871, AMA, Amistad.

[171] Mira Clarke Parsons, "Historic Worthington," *Ohio Archaeological and Historical Publications*, 13 (Columbus, 1904): 71-82; letterhead, Ogden to Cravath, 17 December 1871; flyer, "Ohio Central Normal School, Worthington, Franklin Co., Ohio" [for fall 1873], AMA, 117196, Amistad. "Fourth Annual Catalogue...of the Ohio Central Normal School, 1875-76," (Columbus, 1875) and "Sixth Annual Catalogue...of the Ohio Central Normal and Kindergarten Training School, 1877-78," (Columbus, 1877). *Historical Sketches of the Higher Educational Institutions and also Benevolent and Reformatory Institutions of the State of Ohio*, editor, place, and date unknown, in Ohio Historical Society Library.

Worthington he also undoubtedly kept up an administrative correspondence, much of it mundane. As a change, however, in 1878 he produced a small quasi-scholarly piece called *Outlines of a Complete System of Pedagogical Science, Prepared for the Use of Normal Schools, Normal Classes, Teachers' Institutes, and Private Learners* and a year later he reprinted his major 1858 opus, *The Science of Education and the Art of Teaching*, in two volumes.[172]

While in Worthington Ogden and his wife had their three final children, a boy and two girls, making five in all. Helen Augusta, the last, was born in the spring of 1881, and baptized in Worthington in September which must have been just about when they left the city. During the ten years in Worthington the Ogdens were active in a local church, St. John's Protestant Episcopal, whose Rector, the Reverend Charles H. Young, A.M., was listed as a teacher of Latin and Greek at Ogden's school. Apparently the Ogdens led a contented existence in a pleasant small Ohio city. Ogden's position was one of local respectability and the flavor of this period is of a quiet, bourgeois existence.[173]

During the Gambier and Worthington years Ogden was geographically close to his eldest daughter, Clara Landon Ogden, a young woman (b. 1854) passing into adulthood not far away, in Galion, Ohio. Ogden could see her easily, a convenience he had not known for a dozen years, since before he went to Minnesota, served in the army, and lived in Nashville. In 1875 Clara Ogden married Judge Gilbert Holland Stewart in Worthington and they settled close by in Columbus. Eventually, after her mother's death in 1881, she passed the Ogden family name on to her last son, Donald Ogden Stewart (b. 1894).[174]

---

[172] *Outlines* . . . . Columbus, OH: Gazette Steam Printing House, 1878. 24 p. The 1858 one-volume work now became two volumes: *The Science of Education; or the Philosophy of Human Culture* and *The Art of Teaching*, both Cincinnati, New York: Van Antwerp, Bragg & Co., 1879.

[173] *Shedding Light on Worthington*, Worthington: The Woodrow Guild of the First Presbyterian Church, 2nd ed., 1953; Frank Corbin, *A Walking Tour of Old Worthington* (n.p., 1969), 79-80; *History of Franklin and Pickaway Counties, Ohio* (1880); "Fourth Annual Catalogue of the Ohio Central Normal School, 1875-76," personal communications, Mrs. Evans, St. John's Church, 1976, and Miss Lillian Skeele, Worthington Historical Society, 1976. Ogden Pension Record, 10 January 1899, NA.

[174] In the 1920s Donald Ogden Stewart became an entertaining fiction writer and later a screenwriter. In 1940, as president of two Communist front organizations in Hollywood he battled Congressman Martin Dies of the House Committee on Un-American

One may surmise, based upon hints in John Ogden's Civil War-era poems, that from the late 1850s until Mary Jane Mitchell Ogden's death in 1881 there was considerable tension between her and Ogden. While specific evidence is sparse, one has the sense that she bore a peculiar antagonism to him. The form and character of the tension are nowhere clarified. And the daughter's attitude towards her mother is not clear. Note that her wedding was in Worthington, where her father and stepmother lived, and not in Galion where her mother lived. In later years she seems to have been close to at least one of her much younger half-sisters.[175]

It is not possible to determine how successful—or marginal—the Ohio Central Normal School was financially. Ogden began these Ohio ventures with a minimum of capital, and the timing of his arrival in Worthington was not auspicious. The depression that began in 1873 could not have helped as he and his partners struggled to get or keep the institution on a sound financial basis. Faculty instability appears to have been chronic; no teacher, other than the Ogdens, appears ever to have stayed more than two years. Ogden's departure from Worthington in 1881 was undoubtedly involuntary and relatively sudden for already he had had printed a "Circular of Information No. 1" for the 1881-1882 school year. Probably nothing short of a business failure would have driven him from this reasonably prestigious and comfortable job in a gracious Ohio community near family and friends. The instability and frequent moves that marked the following years indicate that the Ogdens did not leave Worthington because of grand opportunities elsewhere.

Perhaps even the republication of the 1858 text while in Worthington did not represent scholarly eagerness so much as the desire to obtain money from work already done. In any event, Ogden spent ten years in Worthington, by far the longest period that he ever passed in one

---

Activities. Blacklisted after World War II, Stewart moved to England where later appeared his humorous, *By A Stroke of Luck: An Autobiography* (London: Paddington Press, 1975). For an outsider's view of Donald Ogden Stewart see Nora Sayre, *Previous Convictions: A Journey Through the 1950s* (New Brunswick, NJ: Rutgers Univ. Press, 1995), esp. Chap. 25, "Blacklist in Exile." John Ogden's mildly rebellious tendencies thus reappeared more powerfully in his grandson. Wheeler, *Ogden Family*, 379-380; Dennis K. McDaniel, "Martin Dies of Un-American Activities: His Life and Times," (Ph.D. diss., Univ. of Houston, 1988), 421, 452-453.

[175] On 27 July 1891 she inscribed a book (Ruskin's *Sesame and Lilies*) to "Mary Ogden—from her Sister Clara." Book in possession of an Ogden descendant.

location in his working years.

His next position was a one-year principalship (1881-1882) of a fledgling Ohio school, the Fayette Normal, Music, and Business College, located in the village of Fayette, Fulton County, northern Ohio, a few miles from Michigan. The school appears not to have been strong; it had just been founded and the building constructed in 1881. Ogden seems to have had a partner, E. P. Ewers, but as the institution lasted only until 1888 it appears that the move to Fayette was one of desperation for Ogden. Mrs. Ogden did not accompany him there, but apparently taking the newborn, went to Washington, D.C., where Ogden joined her after a year.[176]

When Ogden wound up at Fayette he was fifty-eight years old and to all appearances had come to the end of the string professionally. Although, as we will see, he eventually bounced back surprisingly, for about four years beginning in 1882 he was essentially unemployed and followed his wife to Washington, D.C., where they lived in three different locations. Anna Brewster Ogden, then in her forties, became the main breadwinner. During those years the Washington directories list her as principal for one year of the Garfield Kindergarten (1884), and then both either taught there or had some relationship with it for another year or two. By 1887 a "Kindergarten Training School" was still listed at the address, 923 19th St. NW, where the Garfield Kindergarten had been, but the Ogdens were no longer to be found at that address or anywhere else in Washington.[177]

Ogden's frantic search for activity and income in 1885 is shown in three circulars that he had printed that year. In the first he said that he would be in Dakota Territory in April and offered to select and buy lands there for people for a 5 per cent commission. The second circular proposed a series of thirty-six lectures on education, to be given at the "Martha's Vineyard Summer Institute" beginning 15 July 1885. The third proposed that he, with a partner, would do "Institute Work" in the West in the summer and fall of 1885. He held out the lure that with their

---

[176] Thomas Mikesell, *The County of Fulton* [Ohio], (Madison, WI, 1905), 129-130; Frank Reighard, *A Standard History of Fulton County, Ohio* (New York, 1920), 427-429. Mr. Roger Frazier, Fulton County Historical Society, Wauseon, OH, provided these citations. Larimer, "Evaluation of Ogden," 9.

[177] *Boyd's Director[ies] of the District of Columbia* (Washington, DC, 1882, 1883, 1884, 1885, 1886, 1887). 1882 no entry; 1883, p. 653; 1884, pp. 116, 652; 1885, pp. 120, 650; 1886, pp. 123, 654; 1887, pp. 127, 660.

program an institute could gross as much as $200 per night, a sum that Ogden and his partner proposed to split fifty-fifty with institute sponsors.[178]

It appears that during these years Ogden did sometimes travel to Wisconsin and Minnesota—perhaps only in the summer when he and Mrs. Ogden visited her relatives in St. Paul—or perhaps when passing through to Dakota. The Wisconsin Veterans Museum manuscript dates from the years 1885-1887, and it has evidence of visits to the Twin Cities and involvement in Grand Army of the Republic (G.A.R.) activities.

Given the fact that he had no real position in Washington, D.C., he there conceived the idea that the family ought to go homesteading in Dakota Territory. That Gussie Ogden was willing to go with him, along with the evidence of her dropping from principal to teacher in the Washington kindergarten world, suggests that her own career was not so successful that she could not interrupt it.[179]

The school year 1887-1888 found John Ogden serving as superintendent of schools in McIntosh County, Dakota Territory (subsequently North Dakota). Concurrently, or perhaps a little earlier, he had taken up a "soldier's Homestead" in McIntosh County and while he taught or worked outside the home the family "held" the homestead. The following year Ogden moved a couple of counties over and became principal of the Milnor State Normal School in Milnor, Sargent County, North Dakota. In these years Ogden served frequently as a lay Methodist preacher according to his daughter's testimony.[180]

His occupation for the next year, if any, is uncertain. But in 1890 he was nominated by the North Dakota Republican convention to the office of state Superintendent of Public Instruction. This clearly suggests involvement in the G.A.R., the civil war union veterans organization, because that organization was heavily republican and the Eighties and Nineties were the high points of veteran job-getting through the political

---

[178] Three circulars issued by John Ogden, 923 19th St., N.W., Washington, D.C., 1885. Ogden Papers, in author's possession. See Appendix for full texts.

[179] Bertha R. Palmer, "A Brief History of the Department of Education," (Bismarck, ND, 1932), cited in Larimer, "Evaluation of Ogden," 9, 21-23.

[180] Fragmentary letter, Mary Ogden Larimer to Dorene Heacock Larimer, undated [ca 1932],in Ogden Papers, in author's possession. Nina Farley Wishek, *Along the Trails of Yesterday: The Story of McIntosh County* [North Dakota] (Froh, Pohl, and Monch, ND: The Ashley Tribune, 1940), 400.

process. Ogden won the election, moved to the state capital of Bismarck, and lived there until 1 January 1893. In spite of his age—nearly seventy—he was surprisingly active and innovative in his term as state school leader in North Dakota and there is no indication that he sat back and saw this as a sinecure.[181]

---

[181] Larimer, "Evaluation of Ogden, 21-23; Wishek, *McIntosh County*, 400. Both Dakotas joined the Union in 1889.

CHAPTER 8
Retirement and Old Age in Minnesota and Washington State

Upon the expiration of his term as Superintendent of Public Instruction, the Ogdens immediately left Bismarck, North Dakota, and returned to Minneapolis where Mrs. Ogden reportedly became principal or directress of the Elizabeth Peabody Kindergarten Training School. (The other Twin City was of course her home town.) They spent the next fourteen years together in Minneapolis, she active during a certain number of those years in kindergarten work and he teaching with her, or at least listed as a teacher. In about 1893-1895, on a visit to his daughter and son-in-law in Columbus, Ohio, both Mr. and Mrs. Ogden were celebrated in the local papers—he because he had been a school principal there forty-five years earlier, and she for her kindergarten work in Columbus in the 1870s.[182]

From his Civil War pension applications submitted over several years beginning in North Dakota, one concludes that John Ogden's effective working life ended in December 1892, and that subsequently he had little income except for the veteran's stipend of $35 per month from the Federal government. But Larimer specifically asserts that both were active faculty in the Elizabeth Peabody Kindergarten Training School in Minneapolis from about 1893 until 1907. I have discovered no documentary corroboration. Given their relative ages, however, it is more likely that she remained active longer than he, though she died first.[183]

In the last few years in Minneapolis letters of maudlin sentiment were received and sent, and typical honors were conferred upon Ogden. In 1903 he was made an "Honorable Life Member" of the Minnesota Educational Association. In 1904 Minnesota school teachers sent him gracious birthday greetings and a small monetary gift. In 1908 a former colleague in Bismarck, North Dakota, on behalf of himself and the staff in the state education office, sent "their very kindest regards to dear old Dr. Ogden."

---

[182] Undated clipping, *Ohio State Journal*, [ca. 1893-1895], Ogden Papers, author's possession; Ogden to Cravath, 23 July 1873 [contemporary evidence of Mrs. Ogden's Columbus kindergarten work], AMA, Amistad.

[183] Ogden Pension Record, NA, especially "Declaration for an Invalid Pension," 10 May 1894, and documents dated 14 December 1894 and 10 January 1899.

Fisk University invited him to Nashville for its fortieth anniversary celebration in 1905. (He could not go.) Colonel Oscar H. LaGrange, second commander of the First Wisconsin Cavalry wrote Ogden in 1907 that "I think of you always as I saw you when you reported to me at Cape Girardeau." And LaGrange reported that he had told the regiment at its 1907 reunion in Ripon, Wisconsin, that "Ogden our peacemaker [was a man] whose presence might have lent nobility to base surroundings."[184] These were sure signs that active life was giving way to contemplation of an action-filled time that lay entirely in the past.

In 1907 the Ogdens moved to Seattle, Washington, to be near their children and grandchildren. Mrs. Ogden failed in health and died 12 April 1908 leaving Ogden alone. He died 23 July 1910 and is buried in Lakeview Cemetery in Seattle.[185]

The obituary in the *Westland Educator* aptly summarizes Ogden's life, though today we would place the emphasis elsewhere than was done in Lisbon, North Dakota, in 1910.

JOHN OGDEN

John Ogden, the first president of Winona, Minnesota, State Normal, and State Superintendent of North Dakota from 1890-2, passed away on the 23rd of last July at the home of his daughter, Mrs. Clifford Larimer. Prof. Ogden was born at Crestline, Ohio, February 12, 1824.

The deceased was a prominent educator in the state of Ohio before coming to this state, was a veteran of the Civil War, and after the War assisted in the founding of Fisk University of which he was the first president. He married one of his Winona Normal pupils, Anna Brewster, who was a most excellent kindergartner. The pioneer schoolmen of this state, in particular, deeply mourn the death of this veteran educator.[186]

---

[184] Guy E. Maxwell, Minnesota Education Association, to Ogden, 24 August 1904; Teachers of Minnesota to Ogden, February 1904; C.G. Schulz, Dept. of Public Instruction, State of Minnesota, to Ogden, 12 May 1908; Rev. J.G. Merrill, President, Fisk University, to Ogden, 29 December 1905, all in Ogden Papers, author's possession.

[185] Personal communication, Nancy Pryor, Washington-Northwest Room, Washington State Library, Olympia, 1975. Ogden has many descendants in the Pacific Northwest who have provided leads and copies of material in the family's possession, all of which will eventually be offered to the Amistad Research Center at Tulane University.

[186] *Westland Educator* (Lisbon, ND), September 1910. The birthplace is incorrect.

APPENDIX I

Selected Poems from John Ogden's Civil War Journal

This small selection of poems is presented in chronological order although in his two-volume manuscript journal as it now exists they are in a different sequence, not chronological and not thematic. To judge from the editorial markings, cuts, and small emendations in the text, in later life he toyed with the idea of publishing them, and perhaps even submitted them to publishers.

The more abstractly philosophical poems, or those largely upon religion, I have omitted. They bore such titles as "Life a Mystery", "Good and Evil", "The Trees", and there was a late lamentation from April 1865 called "The Death of Abraham Lincoln." Rather than these topics I wanted to present poems that revealed something of Ogden's attitudes toward the Civil War on the one hand, or his then-wife on the other. In several examples, particularly, "There Shall Be Light in the Evening," the two difficult experiences are treated together in the same poem, in parallel, or as a kind of back and forth. At times during the War Ogden seems to have been uncertain about just what the source of his unhappiness was.

"Thy Will be Done"

I

"They will be done! Thy will be done!"
Be this my prayer though sharp the thorn
That pierces now my wounded side.
Though rough the wave whereon I ride,
My soul shall cry "they will be done!

II

Though grief my spirit overcome
I must not God's great will impugn
And if the fountains overrun
And darkness strangles morn begun
Where hearts now cry—Thy will be done!

III

My flowers are nipped in summer bloom
Sorrow hath found me all too soon.
No *dear one* kneels beside me here!
No *little voice* chimes in my prayers
"They will be done"! "They will be done!"

IV

I kneel beside my bed alone!
I try to pray--I only moan!
For I miss that one sweet voice at prayer
Which always lisped "Our *Father Dear*."
"Thy will be done!" "They will be done!"

V

I miss--Oh God! That chosen one
Who vowed with me life's race to run...
God pity her! She's now grown cold.
But still I'll pray in grief untold
They will be done. Thy will be done!

VI

Bereft of *wife*, of *child*, of *home*
Dear Christ to Thee I come I come!
And while the storm clouds round me roar
My struggling soul cries evermore
Thy will be done, They will be done!

VII

Is there no comfort for me--*none*?
Is hope ashamed? Is faith outdone?
Darkness and doubt encompass me.
Yet to thy bosom, Christ, I flee.
Helpless I cry, They will be done!

VIII

O let us to they bosom turn [?]!
Dear Jesus, take us! Make *us one*
My wife, my child, my own poor heart
As Thou the Son and Father art
The —— God...Thy will be done!

(Verses IX–XXIV omitted)

Cape Girardeau, Missouri
29 September 1862

"DEUS MISEREATUR"
A PRAYER FOR THE PROSPERITY OF THE COURSE OF OUR COUNTRY

God pity our destructed land!
Rent by Secession's bloody hand;
Her reeking garments stained in gore
One surging mass from shore to shore
Her cities wrapped in midnight flame
Proclaim a nation's burning shame
      And lasting infamy.

See how the bloody sword of war
Drinks the red wine of Jenu's car
See how the sons in deadly strife
Lo fratricide doom human life.
While our rank sins have mounted high
The hunt of justice to defy
      In wicked blasphemy.

God hear the cry of those who plead!
The widow's moan, the orphan's need!
Hear for the patriot's earnest prayer
Hear for the Country's wild despair
Hear for the life which Jesus gave
Our race from guilt and sin to save
      A nation purified.

Oh, are there none to intercede?
None like a *Washington* to plead
With sword in hand, for vengeance gain
Lit by the fires of righteous Heaven?
No one to lead out armies forth
As Moses led a conquering host
      To Jordan's swelling tide.

Oh, for a righteous *Livingston*!
The patriot fire of *Lexington*!
The self denying sacrifice!
That pleads for right where justice dies!
That breaks the bar, the prison door!
That liberates God's humble poor
      Where'er they suffering lie!

The wounded maid of Liberty
Her garments rent but hands yet free

Points to the Grave of *Washington*
And asks *Columbia's* noblest son
To bend once more from his abode
And guard this land with freedom's sword
      The sword that's in the sky.

Rouse! rouse ye freemen of the North!
Lead your victorious armies forth!
Strike while the blood of martyrs flows
Strike to the heart of freedom's foes
Strike while the God of battles rides
Forth on the storm with vengeful strides
      To certain victory.

Then guard this land so dearly bought,
This Land for which our fathers fought
This Land baptized in blood and fire
This Land the hope of son and sire
This Land the chosen of the Lord,
Guard it with hand, with pen and sword!
      The Home of Liberty.

Mune [?], Tennessee
June 22, 1863

"THERE SHALL BE LIGHT IN THE EVENING"

I.
The sun that clomb the eastern sky
      Upon the nation's natal morn
Had mounted in the zenith high
      And drank the dew from the lawn.
The sank behind a threatening cloud
That hung the day in nightlike shroud.

II.
A bridegroom stole unseen abroad
      From scenes of mirth–his bridal day-
And sought far from that festal board
      A secret place where he might pray

And there upon the dark green sward
He poured his soul out to the Lord.

III
He prayed that through his fleeting life
      Wisdom might guide his erring feet
And that for her his loving wife
      Joys might in every moment meet
That in that love they crowned that day
They both might live and pass away.

IV
Rising there burst upon his sight
      A scene! 'Twas more than mortal one.
The cloud that hid the glorious light
      Was lumined by the setting sun.
That poured his rays, a golden flood
On cloud, on hill, on vale, on flood.

V
Silent he stood in mute delight
      And gazed upon the parting day;
And as it faded from his sight
      He joyous said, or seemed to say
"So may my days of future life
Close sweetly with my loving wife!"

VI
Days, weeks and months, their wonted sound
      Sped onward in a nation's life.
Fierce struggling passions knew no bound,
      Nor judgement ruled the bitter strife.
The muttering thunders from afar
Gave tokens of approaching war.

VII
A half a score of years had passed--
      I saw that bridegroom not the same.
Time wrought its changes . . . and the last
      In her . . . I weep that change to name!
The love that on the altar burned
Alas to bitter hate had turned!

VIII

I saw him struggling with his grief
   I heard him plead the marriage vow
He agonized to gain relief
   From anguish more than mortal now.
But deeper grew that clouded night
Till darkness shrouded all the light.

IX

Then from his broken soul I heard
   Plaintive and sad, a grief-rung cry.
It was the death of hope deferred!
   It pierced the air, it rent the sky!
Whence faith more radiant still than hope
Thus to that mangled bosom spoke.

"Hope" [a continuation]

(verses I-IV omitted)

V

Then angel of light again spoke
   As she lifted the veil of truth higher.
And she showed him the light that awoke
   Where the sword had devoured, and the fire,
"That <u>these</u> are my children" she said
   "That through suffering and faith have grown bright"
And I saw upon each radiant head
   Rusted crowns and a flame of pure light.

VI

Then I knew that his country and he
   Were struggling together alike
That this suffering alone could make free
   Those that trusted in God and his might.
Then he heard the shrill bugle's loud call
   And the tramp of the squadron in glee;
And he hasted to where freemen fall
   In defense of the land of the free.

VII

I saw him upon the lone march
   In the damps and wilds of the West
Where the hemlocks and poplar and larch
   Build the swamp heron's upon and nest
And still in the faith he was strong.
   And in the first love that he wed

He could not believe he was wrong,
> "There'll be light in the evening," he said.

VIII

I saw him confronting the foe
> And his eyes gleamed unearthly and bright;

For he saw in the battle's fierce glow
> The dawn of that glorious light.

I saw as he dashed in the fray
> The gleam of the purple and red,

But exulting I heard someone say
> "There'll be light in the evening," <u>he</u> said.

IX

Then alone in the forest alone!
> I followed him pensive and sad.

And I heard as he knelt, a deep moan
> For his Country, the joy that he had.

E'er in this deep faith he grew strong.
> When in that first love he had wed;

But he could not believe in the wrong
> "There'll be light in the evening," he said.

X

I saw him in sickness and pain
> As he struggled with want and distress

And this was his joyous refrain
> Like a pilgrim in search of his rest

"My soul, in that Faith be thou strong!
> And in the first Love thou hast wed!

Believe not, Oh believe not in wrong!"
> "There will be Light in the evening," he said.

XI

In prison I found him at length
> Immured for the love that he bore

His Country and those without strength
> For the slave and the suffering poor.

But still in the Faith he was strong
> And in love with his Country instead

He felt in each pulse her deep wrong,
> "But there'll be light in the evening," he said.

XII

"There will be light in the evening," said he
    "When this terrible night shall give way
That hangs o'er my Country and me
    Like a cloud on the eyelids of day
There'll be light in the evening at last
    For home and for Country and me
When the trumpet shall sound a <u>full</u> blast
    And our <u>Land</u> and our <u>Race</u> shall be free."

        In Prison, Macon, Georgia
        June 28th 1864.

Appendix II

Ogden Flyers

LAND FOR THE LANDLESS AND Homes for the Homeless!

THE accompanying papers will answer all questions relating to the right to settle upon Government lands, the means to be employed and the modes of procedure.

It might be further stated, however, that opportunities are frequently offered for investing in other lands, at very low rates, and on long time. The writer expects to be in Hoskins, McIntosh county, Dakota, as early as the 10th of April, 1885, to remain during the summer, excepting a temporary absence east in July, returning again in August, when he will be glad to accompany any who may wish to visit that country.

In addition, therefore, to aiding in the location of Homesteads, Pre-emptions, Soldiers' or Timber Claims in McIntosh county, he will cheerfully undertake the negotiation and purchase of such lands as parties may direct, charging only 5 per cent. on purchase price.

For aiding in the location of Government Claims only such rates will be charged as will cover necessary expenses. For other information, address 923 19th street, Washington, D. C., up to April 1st; after that, till July 1st, Hoskins McIntosh county, Dakota.

JOHN OGDEN.

For cheap railroad rates, see circulars.

JOHN OGDEN,   GEO. E. LITTLE,
Prof. of Teaching.   *Prof. of Drawing. &c.*

JOINT CIRCULARS.

(Supplement)

The above-named parties propose to do such Institute Work, and to give such Entertainments as are described in the accompanying circulars. The proceeds of the latter, which, in some cases have amounted to $200, per night, will be divided equally between the Institute and the lecturer.

They propose to spend the summer and fall of 1885, in the West: and engagements for Teachers' Institutes, Normal Schools, and Colleges, may be made with either or both the parties, direct, or through their agents, as follows:

PRINCIPALS.

John Ogden, 923 19th St., n. w., Washington, D. C.
Geo. E. Little, Cor. 9th & D Sts., n. w., Washington, D. C.

AGENTS FOR WESTERN STATES.

City Supt., B. F. Wright, St. Paul, Minn.
City Supt., H. M. James, Omaha, Nebraska.
Ex-Co. Supt., G. L. Jacobs, Council Bluffs, Iowa.
Supt. Chas. P. Cary, Hamlin, Kansas.

---o---

☞ *For reference, see Testimonials etc. in accompanying Circulars.*

Pencils, Note Books and Blank Drawing Books will be furnished the MEMBERS OF THE INSTITUTE FREE OF CHARGE.

Martha's Vineyard Summer Institute.

(SPECIAL CIRCULAR.)

A Course in Infant Psychology,

The Laws, Growth and Treatment of Early Childhood.

TWELVE LECTURES,

Followed by a *Course* in *Teaching*, (24 Lessons) Commencing July 15, 1885, continuing five weeks.

BY JOHN OGDEN, WASHINGTON, D. C.

The attempt is here made to set forth THE TRUE PHYSICAL AND PSYCHICAL CONDITION OF THE CHILD as the *basis of his right education*.

1. By carefully noting the *natural phenomena* at each successive period of growth.
2. By determining therefrom the *Laws of Maturing Childhood*, the right interpretation of which reveals
3. The *true order of growth*, and the *character of the nourishing supplies*.
4. Whence, THE CHILD'S CONSISTENT TREATMENT IS INFERRED.

This will be done without reference or regard to any pre-existing opinions, or existing systems. It may therefore antagonize some popular notions of schools and education; for, to run a furrow *straight* through this subject, and to make it deep, even to *subsoiling*, will, no doubt, disturb some of our theories of education, "new" as well as old.

But Truth is greater than opinions; and, in a matter of so much importance as the education of a child, I do not see how we can turn aside from the former, even to save the most cherished of the latter.

We therefore invite our fellow teachers to the consideration of some views on this subject, that may not only be new, but full of promise for the children. They have been the result of many years of patient study and experiment.

The foregoing lectures will be supplemented by DAILY LESSONS IN TEACHING, illustrating the principles laid down, as they apply to all grades of children; from which it will be seen that *The Kindergarten* is not the only place where *Scientific Method* can be applied. The whole period of childhood and youth is subject to the same laws of growth.

Special attention will be given to a system of *School Plays and Occupations*, to remedy some existing evils in our popular school management.

These plays and occupations are intended to supplement the "*Busy Work*" in schools—both of which look to the cultivation of health, order, knowledge and efficiency. Only a few of the leading subjects can be given here, under each of which many more can conveniently be grouped, such, for example, as

1. *The Operations of Nature*, as Sunshine and Rain, Wind and Waves, Clouds, Light and Darkness chasing each other around the world, etc.
2. *The Movements, Voices and Habits of Animals*; as in Birds, Beasts, Reptiles, Insects; and even in the growth of Plants.
3. *Employments and Occupations of Men*; as those under Agriculture, Manufactures, Mining, Commerce and Travel, etc.

Under this last general head alone, more than 100 movement plays can be developed, all looking to the cultivation of the bodily powers, and to the acquisition of useful knowledge, and skill.

Here is a field for invention and discovery of immense importance; and it is proposed, at this institute, that suitable premiums be awarded for the best plays and games, their fitness to be determined by a committee appointed for that purpose. Teachers are earnestly requested to give this subject careful consideration. A rational solution to the "*Recess or No Recess*" problem may be found here.

A COURSE OF THIRTY PRACTICAL KINDERGARTEN LESSONS will be given in connection with the foregoing, by MRS. ANNA B. OGDEN, of Washington, D. C., recently in charge of the Kindergarten Work in the *World's Exhibit at New Orleans*. . . . For Tuition, see general circular. Address,

BENJ. W. PUTNAM,
Jamaica Plains, Boston, Mass.

Or, **JOHN OGDEN,**
923 19th St., Washington, D. C.

Appendix III

Inaugural Address of John Ogden, M.A.
Given at the State Normal School, Winona, Minnesota

ADDRESSES

DELIVERED AT THE OPENING OF THE

State Normal School,

WINONA, MINNESOTA,

BY

EDWARD D. NEILL,
Chancellor of University, ex-off. Supt. of Instruction.

AND

JOHN OGDEN, A. M.,
Principal of the School.

WITH

A REPORT

ON THE COURSE OF INSTRUCTION, AND OTHER DOCUMENTS.

PUBLISHED BY THE PRUDENTIAL COMMITTEE.

SAINT PAUL:
PIONEER PRINTING COMPANY.
1860.

Inaugural Address of John Ogden, A. M.

MR CHAIRMAN—LADIES AND GENTLEMEN:—It is customary, on occasions. like this, when an important public enterprise is about to be launched upon the great deep of experiment; or even to be entrusted to the more certain keeping of a tried policy— for those to whom are committed the sacred interests—to give some pledge of fidelity and to make a fair statement of the views and policy, by which they expect to be guided in the management of them.

We cheerfully comply therefore, with this time-honored custom, feeling how important it is, that there should be a thorough and definite understanding, between all parties, before risking such interests as are here at stake.

This day records the organization of the first separate and distinct State Normal School, west of the Father of Waters. And it is needless for me to say, that she launches forth freighted with the dearest hopes, the earnest prayers, and the highest ambition of, at least, the leading minds of the great and free people of the Northwest. And not only so, but other eyes are upon us; and other hearts are beating in sympathy with ours. New Jersey, New York, Connecticut, Massachusetts, Rhode Island, and our nearer relatives are watching this movement, with unusual solicitude. If we shall succeed in making this school what it ought to be, and must be, in fact, to meet the demands of the State, Minnesota will then have won her way to an exalted position among her sister

16

States. Her star, though among the last that has yet arisen in the galaxy of shining orbs, shall not be dim though seen from a distance.

In assuming the charge thus committed to us, by the authorities of the State, we feel that we have an important and double duty to perform—a duty in making known the policy, so as to accomplish the great objects which we have in view, viz: The renovation of the entire educational system of this State, by means of a superior quality of teaching, and to establish it upon a true philosophical basis. The *modus operandi* will be revealed, in part, as our plans are unfolded.

These duties and suggestions distribute themselves as follows:

1. To the Legislative and Executive authorities of this State, by whose wisdom and liberality, means are furnished for putting into operation—and we *humbly trust*—for carrying on this great enterprise to its final completion.

2. To the Honorable Board of Trustees to whom have been committed the proper investment of these means, and the *general* management of the Institution.

3. To the citizens of this State, and particularly to those of this city, by whose foresight and liberality, and in whose midst this Institution has been established.

4. And lastly, to the Teachers and Schools of this State, for whose benefit this wise and liberal provision has been thus early made, and particularly to those Teachers, whose destiny has, this day, been linked with the great common school movement of the North-west, and who are, in a great degree, to be the public exponents of the efficiency and permanency of this enterprise.

1st. *To the Legislature and State Authorities.*—It would seem but courteous, therefore, in assuming the duties thus imposed upon us, by the Board, that due acknowledgement be tendered that body that first conceived and executed the plan, establishing Normal Schools in this State, and above all, to commend that wisdom and liberality by which so large a portion of the public domain is set aside for the exclusive benefits of schools. Three million acres of arable lands, whose value at the present time, cannot be less than $10,000,000, is a sum at once so vast, that it would seem nothing more could have been asked, in this direction, from the general government. Add to the annual income arising from this sum—which in a short time, cannot be less than $1,000,000—with the revenues arising from other sources, and Minnesota can boast a larger school fund than any other State in this Union.

But superior advantages demand superior men and means to manage them. It is pertinent therefore, to inquire how this vast amount can best be expended, so as to meet the demands of the State, and the wants of those for whose benefit it was originally granted. To answer this in full, would involve more discussion and more time, than can here be given. But we might reply briefly, generally, and conclusively, however, by stating that in *no way*, can this amount be expended to greater advantage, than by employing competent and worthy persons to perform the labors and duties for which this expenditure is to be made. This is the only possible solution to the problem; and we submit it for frank and candid consideration. And again, since such laborers cannot be had in sufficient numbers without special provisions for producing them; and since it has been demonstrated time and again in other states, that without competent laborers, the money thus expended is worse than squandered; it does seem desirable, therefore, that some means be devised, both for furnishing competent laborers, and for preventing this fearful public waste. In this way alone, can the original intentions of the framers of the law be carried out. And this seems to be the view now entertained by those in authority. It is safe, therefore, and wise, to suggest, that a very small proportion of this fund be appropriated, as necessity and prudence would demand, for fitting laborers for this great work of educating the children of the State; so that an equivalent may be rendered for this heavy outlay. Here, in the Common School, is where the loss is usually sustained. I call particular attention to this fact. Here, where the money is actually paid out to the laborers, is where the loss falls the most heavily, because *poor* teaching, or *wrong* teaching *is worse than none at all*. And here I would ask, with all candor, would it not be better, and wiser, and safer policy, every way, since the whole fund is virtually at the disposal of the Legislature, at least to be managed by them and their agents, through legal enactments; and since the preparation of teachers for the Common Schools, must and does come, ordinarily within the scope of Common School expense; would it not be better, I say, to invest

18

a small portion of this sum, annually, in training and preparing them for their work, rather than that they should continue in the indifferent discharge of the duties, and receive full pay, without such preparation? Any one can see the wisdom and justice of such a course. It would be the payment of a very small per cent. on the general fund, in order to save it, or to secure its safe and profitable investment. It would be a virtual insurance, with this difference, however, that to the stockholders, in ordinary insurance, nothing but the price of insurance is realized, and this is often reduced by fearful losses, while in the former case, with a proper investment, which this plan proposes to secure, there can be no loss, and the gain is infinitely greater, since whatever is gained in education is infinite; and since every dollar thus expended, in fitting teachers for their duties, besides being instrumental in saving the entire investment, secures twice or thrice the income from the original stock.

Take an example, for instance. Suppose that $500,000 of this fund is to be expended for teaching; and that without properly qualified teachers, as any one can see, the whole of this, or even one half of it ($250,000,) is wasted. And this by no means is an extravagant supposition. But suppose, by the investment of two per cent. of the $500,000, producing a sum equal to $10,000 annually—enough to sustain one good Normal School, and yet only reducing the general fund, per district, about $1,00 annually—that the $250,000—or even the one half of it, $125,000—could be saved annually, what would wisdom dictate in such a case? Why, that it should be done, *of course.* I venture to say, there is not a business man in this city, or in the State, that would manage his own affairs in this way. Here would be a clear saving, according to the lowest estimate, of the difference between $125,000 and $10,000, equal to $115,000 annually, or of twenty-three per cent. per annum on the $500,000.

But when we come to estimate, not only the material losses and gains, but those that relate to the future of the man, then the comparison becomes most alarming. Here, on the one hand, is the loss of time, of opportunity, of talent, of character, of position, of usefulness, of happiness; and not only so, but there is a *positive* injury done the children in the contraction of bad habits, and bad health, bad principles and bad practices, which haunt them like a brood of demons all their days; and on the other hand, the gain of all these, (minus the evils,) with the continually increasing benefits arising from this endless train of good influences. Thus viewed, the convictions are perfectly overwhelming. It does seem that no sane body of men would hesitate for one moment, to make the investment and to make it *liberal*. And this, I rejoice to say, has already been indicated as the future policy of this State and her Legislature.

But it may be asked by some, "Is this a true estimate of these matters, and of the advantages of the Normal School?" We have only time to say, that as far as we have been able to gather information for the last ten years, and to make deductions, it *is* a true estimate, and most emphatically true and significant also; and the statistics of other states will show it most clearly, and our own is beginning to reveal the same startling facts, in reference to poor schools. Every poor school, or school master is a curse; while every good one is a blessing. That is the simple difference. And the sooner we learn that fact, the better.

But again it may be asked, "cannot an ample supply of trained teachers be had from other institutions, and from other sources?" We can only say to this, that they never have been yet, in any single instance, either in this country or any other: and they never *can* be had in sufficient numbers, and of proper qualifications, from those sources; simply because other institutions concern themselves mainly about the qualifications of their pupils for other and ulterior objects. You might, ladies and gentlemen, as reasonably expect, that broom manufactories would yield a sufficient supply of tailors or cobblers; or that the study of the classics would furnish an ample supply of doctors or lawyers. "Like produces its like." "The stream can rise no higher than the fountain." The broom manufactory will produce brooms and broom makers, and not tailors. The classics will make scholars and not doctors. And the Normal School, when it *is* a Normal School, will produce teachers; and no other institutions can, to the same extent, until they are organized and conducted on the same plan; and when that takes place, then they become Normal Schools. Hence it is idle to look for a supply of highly trained and efficient teachers, outside of the means whereby they are produced. Teaching is just as distinctly, essentially, and emphatically a profession, to be learned by observation, study and practice, as any other.

20

But we have no time to pursue this subject further here. We close this part of it therefore, by stating what all will admit to be true, viz: that for whatever grants made to the Normal School, either for buildings, apparatus or other purposes, a full equivalent should be rendered in properly qualified teachers. The State has a right to expect this; and hence the Legislature has wisely provided, that in consideration of this, she has a claim on the services of the teachers here instructed, for at least two years after entering the Institution. And here let me assure that honorable body, and all others concerned in this matter, that *no candidate for such services, shall ever leave this Institution with my official sanction, until he or she, shall have rendered good evidence of such qualifications, physically, intellectually, and morally, as shall meet the demands of the schools and the State.*

I am aware that Normal Schools have not always met public expectation, in this respect. I am also aware that they have not always done their duty. But the failure has been more the result of inadequate means, poor organization, and mismanagement, and misdirected efforts, than from any radical defect in the system itself. The effort has been, too much, to meet a demand that should be met in the common school and higher seminaries of learning, viz: the literary qualification alone, of teachers. Hence Normal Schools have degenerated in some instances, into mere academies. But this can be shown to be entirely unnecessary. Their duties are as distinctive in their scope and characteristics, as those of any other professional school. Their office is, not merely to make scholars, but *teachers.* And here, we would be willing to pledge the State an ample supply of them, provided it will furnish the material from which to manufacture them, and the means whereby to operate. And we repeat, that in no other way can this great want, on the part of the State, be met, in that truest and highest sense, except by establishing Normal Schools, where the teachers may learn the *science,* and be trained in the *art* of teaching. But we have no time to pursue this subject here. Other reasons will be revealed as we proceed.

2nd. *The Board of Trustees.*—Gentlemen: Allow me to address you personally on this occasion; and thank you for the distinguished honor you have conferred upon me, in thus committing to my care, the direction and management of this school. I feel,

21

Sirs, in accepting this position, that I have accepted at your hands, a holy trust, and a life labor. Surely, to carry out your views, as they have been expressed to me, and as I conceive they ought to be carried out, would require, not the sacrifice of a life, but the success of one. Not only care, and toil, and selfdenial, and labor —man's best inheritance here—are involved in this struggle, but the rewards, the triumphs, the conquest, the glory, the fulfillment of our devoutest expectations, the consummation of our dearest hopes, viz: the development and sublimation of man's highest powers, in devotion to a cause, that looks not at the present good alone; but away, far beyond, to the happiness of the unborn millions of our race. All this, and much more, is involved in the labors which we this day inaugurate.

It is but natural that I should feel the weight of this responsibility, and my great incompetency for a work so vast and overwhelming. But duties so arduous, so exalted, so ennobling, and so divine, I confess, have great and strong attachments. And with your counsel, your sympathy and your labors, I shall devoutly accept them, trusting humbly in Divine wisdom for that guidance which alone can ensure safety and success. And while it shall be my earnest desire, and my happiness, at all times, to acquiesce in your views, and to carry out your wishes, it will readily be seen by you, that the internal management of the school must be entrusted to an individual mind; must be a unity; and that unity is best exemplified in the individual decisions and acts of the representative head, aided, of course, by those whom you may place in the school as assistants, which assistants should be the united choice of yourselves and the Principal. This faculty must be left entirely untrammeled in the exercise of those functions exclusively internal, and at the same time, allowed a liberal share of suggestive latitude in the general management.

I feel, Gentlemen, in common with yourselves, that the Normal School must succeed; that it must accomplish the great object for which it was formed, to wit: the renovation and purification of the entire education enterprize of this State; that the greatest good to the greatest number must be its high object and aim. And if I see that its success depends upon the sacrifice of personal ease, personal favor, or the opinion of personal friends, *person* " must stand from under." The Normal School, first, last, and all

22

the time. Its interests are too sacred to barter at any price. They are inseparably linked with all the common schools of this State. The success of the Normal School must be the success of common schools, directly, or indirectly. They live and breathe together. Any thing, therefore, tending to engender prejudice and local strife, must injure the Normal School, since its life, its instincts, its usefulness and nourishment all depend upon the favor in which it is held by the popular masses, whose servant it is. Let it spread wide its arms, and strike deep its roots, and embrace all that comes, legitimately, under the name of school or education. Far be it from you, or from me, to consent to use the liberality of the State, for the aggrandizement of a merely local interest. The State Normal School should be linked with no such faction; but should be looked after and built up at the sacrifice of every other interest, let that be merely local or otherwise.

This brings us to notice, in the third place, the relations and obligations existing between this school and the citizens generally, and those of this place more especially. Every citizen in this broad land has a sacred and inalienable right to a part of the public domain, and especially to that portion of it which is set aside for the education of the children. If he has no children, so much the worse for him. That is his misfortune, and goes just that far towards rendering him a useless member of society. But this, by no means, releases him from the obligation of expending his portion of such domain for the education of his neighbors' children; since his own personal interests, by virtue of his partial isolation, are identified with theirs, and are advanced proportionally with theirs, and the general good. He ought to expend it all the more willingly, since he reaps the common benefits of society, without contributing anything to its membership; and since he enjoys all the immunities thereof, without expense, save the little he gives, in common with his neighbors, for the public weal.

Another truth equally selfevident, is that every child, white, red or black, male or female, bond or free, rich or poor, high or low, domestic or foreign, has an inalienable right to an education. No laws nor law makers have any more right to deprive children of this, than they have to break their arms or legs, or to put out their eyes. And on the same principle, we assume that the laws are deficient, and lawmakers are culpable, just to the extent that they do not provide for the thorough education of the children of the State. Since in failing to do this, they entail worse than merely physical evils upon them and the State, by depriving the former of the free use of all their legitimate powers, and the State of their services. Again, by the infliction of merely physical injury, the damage, for the most part, is only temporal; but in the former case, whether from neglect or otherwise, it is not only temporal, to a more fearful extent too, but it is also eternal, and self-perpetuating, since it is entailed upon future generations. We claim, therefore, that this education is a most sacred inheritance, to which the child is born, and of which no earthly power should divest him.

And further, this education should be free—as free as the air he breathes; and to all classes alike accessible, so far, at least, as the distribution of the public fund is concerned. We are prepared to defend the doctrine, "that the property of the State should educate the children of the State;" (and that includes the teachers of the State also,) and that this, so far from weakening the parental obligation to educate, only strengthens it, and renders it more practical and certain.

But how does this doctrine effect the Normal School, and its obligations to the State? Much every way; but chiefly, in that it points out the mutual relationship and dependencies existing between them, every man and woman, whether parent or not; every boy and girl in this broad State, has an interest in this Normal School. That interest is indefeasible, and co-extensive with the expenditures and the benefits. Its blessings like its expenses, therefore, should be distributed, as far as possible, to all alike.

But while its benefits are thus distributed, it cannot escape you, fellow citizens, that the obligations are also mutual. Its separate and isolated existence, as a Normal School, is simply impossible. It must derive its prosperity and consequent usefulness, mainly from the generous support you give its pupils. These teachers will be asking for schools, by and by, that they may give an equivalent, for the assistance they have received from the State. Thus you will perceive that the State has made you her agents, through whom she expects her remuneration. And while it is not expected that you are under any special obligations to employ these when you can get others equally as good, or better, (if that were possible,) for less money; yet it is expected that you will not allow them to be pushed aside and crowded out by those who are less qualified, because they can afford to "*teach cheap.*" No; your own interests, as well as the deference you should show the wise provisions of the State, would forbid this.

I will not stop here to discuss the ruinous policy of employing "cheap teachers," because they *are* cheap, further than to say, that those "cheap teachers" are the dearest in the end; since they render the State no equivalent for the miserable salaries they eke out of her Treasury. To employ poor teachers for poor schools, is the surest way to keep them poor. To employ illiterate teachers for backward schools, is like employing the poorest doctors for the sickest patients. "They that are whole, have no need of the physician, but they that are sick." As a general thing, we need the best teachers for the poorest schools. I will not say *best* in every point of qualification; but *best* for that particular school—the best adapted for its peculiar wants. No one, therefore can fail to see the propriety of employing the best teachers, in point of professional ability, for the primary schools; since it requires more wisdom, greater experience, and a rarer gift to instruct and control small children, than any others. And this importance is very much heightened, when we take into the account the character and durability of the impressions made in early life. But this teaching gift is cultivable, and is peculiar to a certain class, mostly females. And the natural gift, without cultivation of it, is often worse than no gift, since it confers additional power, without the ability to control, and direct in useful channels. Hence, the very great importance of employing female teachers that have been trained in the Normal School, where opportunities have been enjoyed for the study of this subject in all its phases, and for witnessing and testing the best method of teaching children of all grades and ages. And this importance increases in proportion to the number of these teachers that are annually employed in the public schools of the State.

This brings us to notice, in this connection the character and organization of the Normal School, more at length; giving its peculiar fitness for supplying just such teachers as the schools of the State may require, as a *desideratum* of the very first importance.

We cannot here enter into a description of the organization and wants of these schools, further than to say that with a competent

25

teacher, we believe every district school, and indeed, almost every other, may be classified into three general divisions, and each of these into two or three sub-divisions, or classes. In cities and larger towns, classification is still more readily effected by establishing what are called *Graded Schools*, including Primary, Secondary, Grammar and High School. The last one of these grades is seldom if ever required in the country school, while all three of the other departments, will, in most cases, be represented in the same school.

Now each of these classes or divisions will require separate and distinct characteristics in teaching. It is necessary, also, that under these circumstances, they all shall be combined in one and the same teacher. Or in other words, the teacher will be required to teach a Primary, Secondary, and Grammar School, all at the same time and in the same school room. And this, my friends, is the great perplexing question, *to-day*, in the thorough and consistent organization of the country district school. The Normal School must meet and grapple with this difficulty. It must meet it fairly, and as far as possible, provide a remedy for it; for it is for this purpose chiefly, viz: to prepare teachers for the common schools, that it has been established.

In order, therefore, to accomplish this object, there must be an organization of its several departments looking to these several difficulties, and at the same time accomplishing the other objects of a Normal School. The whole system, therefore, presupposes the existence of a model or experimental school, in connection with the other departments, in which all these types of school can be represented. The mixed-grade school, or the one having three or four grades, in the same room, as described above, I believe has never yet been attempted in the Normal School. The others have, with the most satisfactory results. And I see no good reasons why this one may not also be organized with like results. The Normal School would then present a complete system, representative of the entire educational machinery of the State, both as to classified and unclassified schools. And this is what it should do. It does not fulfill its mission unless it does thus represent it. Here then, in addition to other advantages, the pupil—teacher—may study the entire system of graded schools from the highest to the lowest department, and become familiar with the management of all these several grades and classes.

But it might be well, further to describe this *model*, since the efficacy of the Normal school, and hence the benefits arising to citizens from its location here, will depend in a great measure, upon the perfection of this organization.

First in order then, we should have the Normal School proper, including the Normal or Professional Department, and the High School, or Preparatory Department. These departments are both necessary to the efficiency and existence of the Normal School, and hence should have their location in the same building. The Academic Course can then be made as thorough as most Collegiate Courses, and much more disciplinary and practical.

Second.—The Grammar School Department, one Secondary, (grade *a*,) and the mixed or rough grade, should occupy another, and adjacent building. These departments, as has just been shown, are also necessary to the thorough organization of a representative system of education for a state or a community.

And third and lastly, there would be the other secondary grade, (*b*,) and the two Primary Departments, (grades *a* and *b*,) to occupy a building similar to the one for the Grammar School, etc.

The above arrangement proceeds upon the supposition that three buildings be provided, in time for the accommodation of this system of schools, or all three of these departments slightly modified, might occupy the same building, if it were of sufficient size. The whole, then would read thus, arranged with reference to entire grades and departments: one Normal Department, one High School Department, one Grammar School Department, one Secondary Department, including grades *a* and *b*, one miscellaneous grade, and one Primary Department, including grades *a* and *b*. Other departments and grades could be established, if the number in attendance and circumstances require it.

Now each one of these departments should be superintended by a Principal, and each one of the grades by a permanent teacher, who, according to the following arrangement, would be able to take charge of from one hundred to two hundred and fifty pupils. Each one of these departments would be sub-divided into a convenient number of classes, according to the age, capacity and attainments of the pupils. There should also be from four to six class or recitation rooms attached to each one of the main rooms in these buildings. Each department would then be provided with one large assembly or study room, arranged so as to seat two hundred pupils, and six class rooms, adjoining, for recitation. In this large room, all the general exercises could be conducted, and all study and preparation made, when, at given times and signals, the classes may retire to their several recitation rooms, where they are met by two select classes of Normal pupils, two for each room, one from the junior class, as an observer, and one from the senior class as teacher, or this may be varied to suit circumstances.

Now then, Normal pupils, (those of them who give instruction) must first have undergone a thorough training and preparation in the Normal School, on the lessons to be taught, and must also have undergone an examination on the most approved modes of teaching, before they are permitted to take charge of classes. The others come in as mere observers, to note the methods of instruction, and to learn the disposition and advancement of the pupils; so that they, when their turn comes, may be able to carry the instruction forward without interruption.

These classes are here drilled thoroughly for the required time, when their places are supplied, it may be, by another class and other teachers. The teaching will be supplied, either by the Principal of the Normal School, the Principal of the Department, or the head teacher in the class. And during the absence of any teacher from his department, his place can be supplied from the teaching class of Normal pupils, when and where another very important "school-room duty" can be learned and practiced, viz: the art of governing the school, securing study, and managing the whole machinery at intervals.

Here then, in this system, teaching may be learned in the only successful way, and in all departments and grades of school. And it is astonishing, the amount of it, that may be done; and the perfection to which the teaching and learning may be brought, under an arrangement of this kind. The Model School is the only true type of school.

1st. Because *it fulfills the conditions of education more nearly than any other*, since the exercises of study, recitation and teaching are distributed in about the right proportion among all grades—teachers as well as pupils—thus affording a harmonious and consistent blending of all the forces of education, of acquisition and use, the true interchangeable relation of want and supply.

2nd. Because *it costs less money to teach the same number of pupils;* since each paid teacher or principal may safely superintend two hundred pupils, if need be, being assisted each day by a corps of from four to six trained pupil teachers, who teach without compensation, as a part of their Normal School training. Making the expense about one-half or one-third less for the same amount and quality of teaching.

3rd. Because *it secures better teachers, every way;* since those who superintend must themselves be first class teachers, which gives character to all the teaching, in all the classes, and all the departments. 2. Since the pupil teachers must themselves have spent one week or more, in observing methods and studying the disposition and capacity of the class, and have undergone a thorough examination as to preparation of the lessons and other exercises to be taught, before they are allowed to give instruction in class. 3. Because they have an additional motive for thoroughness, since their standing in the Normal School is determined from their record of teaching, more than from that of learning what to teach. 4. Since the classes may be smaller, and more evenly graded; this being one of the chief advantages, since a most thorough and consistent grading of all the pupils may thus be secured. 5. Since from three to four times as much time and attention may be devoted to the individual classes and pupils as there can be under the ordinary arrangement. 6. Since by this method, we are able to keep the pupils busy all the time, at some appropriate employment or exercise, and thus prevent that bane of all schools and all society, *idleness,* which is doing more to-day to curse our schools, than any other one thing, since the pupils, in the great majority of instances, spend from one-half to three-fourths of their time in doing nothing at all, or worse than nothing; and these habits carry themselves right into their business of whatever character, in after life. Now this can be prevented or removed, only by some such arrangement as described above, by which all the time of the child may be employed. Other advantages might be named; but we pass to notice in the next place,

The advantages of this arrangement to the pupils of the Normal School, and hence to the other schools of the State, through them.

1st. It affords an opportunity to the pupil teacher to study the whole system of graded schools, from the lowest to the highest department, in one comprehensive *model*.

2nd. It affords him an opportunity to witness the organization, government, recitations and other exercises, conducted on the most approved plans.

3rd. It affords him just what every young teacher should have before he is intrusted with a school of his own, viz: an opportunity to direct and manage the *studies* of children, as well as to give instruction; and in fact, to assume the entire responsibility for the conduct of the school for a given time.

4th. It affords an opportunity to any teacher who may desire it, to cultivate his or her particular talent for any particular grade of school.

5th. It affords the same opportunity to any who may wish to qualify themselves for all the grades of school; since they can enter any one of these particular grades, as an actual practitioner, and pass successively through the whole.

6th. And superadded to these advantages, the teacher, during this term of observation and practice, is to study the educational system of the State, the science of education in general, and making himself familiar, not only with the school laws of the State, but with the laws of human growth and culture, the capacity of all the human powers, the nature and force of the various departments of science, their fitness for the several educational purposes, and thus laying the foundation for a successful career as a professional teacher.

It will be seen from the above, what the Normal school is capable of doing, provided it can rely upon you, my friends, and upon the Legislature for the necessary aid. Just such a school is needed for the State purposes, and just such a school may be established in your city if you desire it. The State needs what you can most consistently commit to her, and you need what the State can most consistently commit to you. The advantages shall therefore be natural and self-perpetuating; and the expense, by virtue of this accommodation and division of labor, may be greatly reduced to both parties.

Our Normal School must prove, at best, but a medium affair, unless we can have the means in time, for putting it into full play, in all its parts. It must forever be a cripple, if we allow it to grow up deformed or defective in any of its departments. No one can fail to see that a school of this kind is the great educational necessity of the State. As such, it makes its appeal to us this day for aid. Colleges and Universities are luxuries which we do not specially need just now, Normal Schools, or the preparation of teachers, for the schools of the State, is the *necessity*, I repeat, which must be met now, or the defeat of Colleges, Universities and every other institution is rendered doubly certain.

I confess, fellow citizens, I have long wished for an opportunity for putting into operation my cherished ideas of schools and education—an opportunity for establishing a *model*, consistent and adequate, in all its parts, and adapted to the great wants of a State.

May I not look with encouragement to your State, and to your city for the necessary advantages? Will you afford me that long coveted opportunity, or must I look elsewhere? I trust you will not thrust aside these countless advantages described above, and suffer your schools, and the school system of the State, to be trampled down by ruthless speculation, or the equally destructive agencies of indifference and neglect. Let Minnesota utter her voice on this important subject. Let her broad and fertile prairies, her beautiful valleys and fields, her boundless resources of wealth, answer. Let a voice from the legislative halls answer. Let a voice from the peaceful citizens answer. Let that pleading voice that comes up from her children in every city, town, and hamlet, and from every school-house, and all these utterances, be heard and heeded. Unless they are, the mingled din of those voices will rise, ere long, again, borne on every breeze across our lakes, rivers and plains, more plaintive now, more clamorous, more discordant, more imperative, more terrible, pleading for more asylums, more courts, more missions, more money, more bread; and we must answer this call with our cash. There will be no escape then; and the penalty will be the more unwelcome and more fearful, since it might have been prevented.

4. But we come now to notice, in the last place, some of the peculiarities of a Normal School, as distinguished from other institutions. The relation it sustains to those institutions, to teachers generally, and especially to those who are present this day as pupils. The first we must allude to but briefly.

31

What we mean by other institutions in this connection, is the entire educational machinery of the State, whether benevolent or otherwise. The educational influences are not bounded by the precincts of the Common School, however general and powerful these schools may be made; but they extend as far and wide as the influences of man can extend. The asylums for the deaf and dumb, the blind, the insane, the idiotic or imbecile; houses of refuge or reform, benevolent societies, Sabbath schools, churches, and even down to that most potent of all educators, the family and social circle—all these, and many more, are the fit subjects for the study and labor of the Normal pupil.

My young friends, when you enter this field, you not only pledge yourselves the public servants of the State, but you enter a missionary field, in the highest and truest sense of that term. You ally yourselves and your fortunes with the dearest interests of the State—with every thing in fact, that is holy, ennobling and good, with that endless chain of mighty influences that links man to his Maker. You penetrate that great deep of unseen causes and influences, which evermore surges with the burden of our broken and shattered humanity. You lay your hands upon Divine things, and solemnly pledge yourselves to handle them as the instruments of God, for the restoration of the lost loveliness to the soul, the clearness and vigor to the intellect, and the health and manliness to the human form divine. You should tremble as you enter this holy sanctuary—the holiest in the records of the human family—the sanctuary of thoughts, emotions, volitions, and God-like power—a sanctuary all redolent with the divinest aroma—the living, moving, deathless energies of human souls. And, as Moses was commanded to put off the shoes from his feet, in the visible presence of the Burning Bush, should you, as you enter here, divest yourselves of every unholy thought, feeling and desire; and arm yourselves with that innocence and purity that made Satan stand aghast, gnashing, and acknowledge, when angel-confronted, and touched by Ithuriel's spear, "how awful goodness is." Thus, my young friends, should you equip yourselves, as you enter this arena, where passions sometimes strive for power; but where discipline chastens and refines them, and makes them the obedient servants of the will. Thus should you surround yourselves with those heavenly guards, innocence and virtue, that you may walk

32

through the furnace of trials, conflicts and temptations incident to an educational career, without even so much as the smell of fire upon your garments. Then shall ye be strong, through Christ the strength of all sound education, to do battle against the hosts of ignorance and sin. But we have only time to call your attention to some of the leading characteristics of this school, and to some of the obligations resting upon you, by virtue of your espousal of this cause to-day.

In the first place, then, this is no ordinary school. By its very name and profession, it takes a higher stand than other institutions. Not higher, perhaps, in a literary sense; but higher in that it assumes the prerogative to give directions and instruction in the use of knowledge, and every other instrument for the elevation of the race. It is professional. While other institutions propose to develop the human faculties, by the acquisition of knowledge; this proposes more. It professes also to teach and enforce the right application of this knowledge, and this human power, thus generated and developed, to the development of similar qualities in others. And its character, consequently, ranks as much higher than that of ordinary institutions, in these respects, as the application or use of knowledge is higher than the mere acquisition of it. Its regime of study, discipline and labor must, therefore, rank correspondingly high, or it does not fulfil its mission. Every one's progress here, must be measured by his ability to use knowledge skillfully in teaching others. In most institutions the pupil studies to *know;* here he studies to *do.* It will be seen, therefore, that this school will be no place for idleness or wickedness; for there will be no time for the indulgence of these propensities. Idleness is incompatible with the genius of the Normal School. Indeed, it cannot exist, without a flagrant violation of the conditions of membership. A lazy person never ought to come in sight of children—save as a warning—much less should he teach them. Laziness will no more be tolerated here, than drunkenness and kindred vices.

Again, wickedness will not be tolerated here. I use the comprehensive term wickedness to denote all vice and crime, and every thing that leads to them. The warfare shall therefore be as sore against wickedness as against ignorance. I never could reconcile the inconsistency of a person's educating a part of himself at a time; or a part of himself for good and a part for evil. "No man can serve two masters." We shall proceed therefore upon the plan of educating a whole man at a time, well knowing that in order to produce harmonious results, there must be a harmonious and consistent blending of all the influences and exercises necessary to produce those results. Neither can I reconcile the inconsistency of an educated man's being a bad man, any more then I can a sick man's being a well man, a weak man's being a strong man, or a wise man's being a fool. Education means the development of all the possible good in men, and the suppression of all the possible evil. It is a renovation and restoration of all his original powers, to a comparative state of purity, activity, and vigor, wrought out through the heaven-appointed means for restoring to man what was lost, when he basely yielded up those powers, to the disobedience and sin that wrought such ruin among them. But every educational want has its corresponding supply: and every disease of body, mind and soul, has its antidote. Hence that education that does not recognize Christ in it—the great antidote for sin—is no education, in the truest sense of the word; since it ignores the only life-giving principle from which all true progress springs. He alone can neutralize sin, that primal cause of all physical, intellectual and moral obliquity, which an education seeks to correct, and put man's powers into a true condition of growth and development.

A man's real education begins with a new birth. But Nicodemus said, "How can these things be?" So will many other blind Pharisees of the present day, imagine; but the truth stands there nevertheless: and just so long as we ignore it, we shall fail, as we deserve to fail, in the true education of the race. We may build school-houses and plant colleges, and universities, and Normal Schools, until our land is clouded with them, and we shall forever fail until we recognize this one simple truth. I say, therefore, a man's real education begins with a new birth. All antecedent to this is preparatory, and should be directed with strict reference to this one great event, when he can begin to grow and drink in the great truths of science and religion. A man can only grow harmoniously when he grows in accordance with God's plan of growth. His plan is that he shall grow in goodness as fast as he grows in wisdom, and that his physical powers shall not be interfered with, but strengthened and refined in this, and by this growth. How then can an educated man be a bad man? He cannot, any more than light can be darkness, or good can be evil, or virtue, vice; for whatever he lacks of being good, or what God designed he should be, he lacks in his education. And the same is true in every other possible respect. Whatever he lacks of filling the measure of manhood, in a physical, intellectual, moral and spiritual sense, as marked out by the Creator, he lacks in his thorough full-orbed development, as a man, a Christian, a scholar, an *educator*.

I cannot consent, therefore, to any other definition, interpretation or application of education, than that which looks to the accomplishment of all these objects, in the fullest and highest sense. And here allow me to add, that no teacher can pass under the sanction of this Institution, who does not possess all these attributes, if not in a high, at least in a respectable degree. The spirit and letter of the laws of the land, bear testimony to the soundness and safety of this position. I would not turn a bear or a wolf loose among a flock of lambs; neither would I, a teacher, with a bad heart, bad morals, bad principles, and *bad practices*. Much less then, would I turn him loose among little children, and schools, and then add to his license my official sanction. I thus make myself responsible for the evil he may do.

A fool cannot teach wisdom; neither can a bad man teach goodness, except in a negative way. Satan cannot correct sin; therefore, his emissaries should not be employed to cultivate the vineyards of the Almighty, where so much sin and moral obliquity are to be dealt with. Knowledge and goodness grow best together. Therefore, no attempt to separate them should be tolerated. Religion and science were made to go hand in hand. Their mission is the redemption of the race. "What, therefore, God has joined together, let not man put assunder."

Well, which do we need most, to-day, knowledge or goodness? Intellectuality or spirituality? Smartness or honesty? Shrewdness or integrity? Half men or whole men? Men without souls or with souls? These questions properly answered, and then we shall be able to determine the character of the teaching most needed.

Nay, my fellow teachers and pupils, education and teaching

mean more than merely hearing recitations and keeping good order. They mean building up human bodies, minds and souls, each in one harmonious, majestic, living, temple; and adorning it with all that is beautiful, costly, pure and good.

But our space here* only allows us to add in conclusion, that it shall be the leading object of the Normal School, so to distribute its labors and other exercises, that all the faculties of the pupil teacher, physical, intellectual, moral and spiritual, shall be addressed in due proportion, at the proper time, and in the proper manner; and so to develop, strengthen, elevate and purify these powers, in the student; and so to train him in the educational processes, that he may readily apply them to the education of the children and youth committed to his care. More pains shall be taken to make teachers, than mere scholars; well knowing this to be the point upon which Normal Schools fail more frequently than upon any other. Here then, fellow teachers and friends, in this brief outline, behold my ideal of a school. Behold my type of a National Education. Behold what your schools ought to be, and every school must be, if we ever expect to meet a tithe of that weighty obligation resting upon us, the public servants of this great and growing Commonwealth.

---

* Only a small part of the fourth head of this address is published for want of space.

Bibliography

PRIMARY SOURCES

American Missionary Association, *Annual Reports*, 1866-1871.
American Missionary Association Archives, Amistad Research Center, Tulane University.
Barnard Papers, Fales Library, Bobst Library, New York University.
    Civil War Small Collections, John Ogden file, Wisconsin Veterans Museum, Madison.
Daniels, Edward, Papers. Archives-Manuscript Division, State Historical Society of Wisconsin, Madison.
Ogden, John, Papers. Amistad Research Center, Tulane University.
    National Archives.
    Bureau of Refugees, Freedmen, and Abandoned Lands, Record Group 105. (National Archives Microfilm Publication M999.)
    Compiled Records Showing Service of Military Units of Volunteer Union Organizations. (National Archives Microfilm Publication M594.)
    Ogden, John, Military Pension Record. 1st Wisconsin Cavalry. Civil War.
    Ogden, John, Military Record, Companies M and E, 1st Wisconsin Cavalry, Civil War.
Neill, Edward Duffield, and John Ogden, *Addresses Delivered at the Opening of the State Normal School, Winona, Minnesota, With a Report on the Course of Instruction, and Other Documents*. Saint Paul, 1860.
Taylor, Alrutheus A., Fisk University, 1866-1951: A Constructive Influence in American Life." Unpub. Manuscript, Amistad Research Center, Tulane University.
War of the Rebellion: A Compilation of the Official Records of the Union and Confederate Armies 69 vols and Index. Washington, 1880-1901.

SECONDARY SOURCES

ABBOTT, A. O., ed., *Prison Life in the South: At Richmond, Macon, Savannah, Charleston, Columbia, Charlotte, Raleigh, Goldsborough, and Andersonville During the Years 1864 and 1865*. New York, 1865
AMERICAN MISSIONARY ASSOCIATION, *American Missionary*. New York, 1865-1871.
AMERICAN MISSIONARY ASSOCIATION, *History of the American Missionary Association*. New York: American Missionary Association, 1891.
ARMSTRONG, WILLIAM H., *A Friend to God's Poor: Edward Parmelee Smith*. Athens: University of Georgia Press, 1993.
BARTLEY, W. W., "What Was Wrong with Darwin?," *New York Review of Books*, 24:14 (15 Sept. 1977).
BEARD, AUGUSTUS F., *A Crusade of Brotherhood*. New York, 1972; first pub. 1909.

BENTLEY, GEORGE R., *A History of the Freedmen's Bureau.* New York, 1974; first pub. 1955.

BLEDSTEIN, BURTON J., *The Culture of Professionalism: The Middle Class and the Development of High Education in America.* New York, 1976.

BOND, HORACE MANN, *The Education of the Negro in the American Social Order.* New York, 1934.

Boyd's Directory of the District of Columbia. Washington, DC, 1882-1887.

BUTCHART, RONALD E., "Educating for Freedom: Northern Whites and the Origins of Black Education in the South, 1862-1875," Ph. D. dissertation, State University of New York–Binghamton, 1976.

―――――, *Northern Schools, Southern Blacks, and Reconstruction: Freedmen's Education, 1862-1875.* Westport, CT, 1980.

CARTER, DAN T., *When the War Was Over: The Failure of Self-Reconstruction in the South, 1865-1867.* Baton Rouge: Louisiana State University Press, 1985.

Colored Tennessean, The, weekly, ca. April 1865–1866. Beginning 1866, called *The Tennessean.*

CORBIN, FRANK, *A Walking Tour of Old Worthington,* N.p., 1969.

CURRY, J. L. M., *A Brief Sketch of George Peabody, and a History of the Peabody Education Fund Through Thirty Years.* New York, 1969; first pub. 1898.

CURTI, MERLE, *The Social Ideas of American Educators.* New York, 1935.

DRAKE, RICHARD B. "American Missionary Association and the Southern Negro, 1861-1888." Ph.D. dissertation, Emory University, 1957.

DUBOIS, W. E. B., *The Autobiography of W. E. B. DuBois.* New York, 1968.

―――――, *Dusk of Dawn: An Essay Toward an Autobiography of a Race Concept.* New York, 1940.

ECKELBERRY, R. H., "The McNeely Normal School and Hopedale Normal College," *Ohio Archaeological and Historical Publications* , 50 (1931): 86-136.

Edgefield Advertiser. Edgefield, South Carolina.

ELSON, RUTH MILLER, "American Schoolbooks and 'Culture' in the Nineteenth Century," *Mississippi Valley Historical Review,* 46 (December 1959).

FONER, ERIC, *Reconstruction: The Unfinished Revolution, 1863-1867.* New York, 1988.

GILLETTE, WILLIAM, *Retreat from Reconstruction, 1869-1879.* Baton Rouge: Louisiana State University Press, 1979.

GLEASON, GENE, "The Wanderer: Racing Yacht to Slave Ship," *Southern Exposure,* (March/April 1984): 59-62.

GLAZIER, WILLARD W., *The Capture, The Prison Pen, and the Escape.* New York, 1868.

HARROLD, STANLEY, *Gamaliel Bailey and Antislavery Union.* Kent, Ohio: Kent State University Press, 1986.

HERBST, JURGEN, *And Sadly Teach: Teacher Education and Professionalism in American Education.* Madison, 1989.

HERRMANN, WILLIAM H. *The Rise of the Public Normal School System in Wisconsin.* Madison: University of Wisconsin Press, 1971.

HESSELTINE, WILLIAM, *Civil War Prisons: A Study in War Psychology*. New York, 1965; first pub. 1930.
History of Franklin and Pickaway Counties, Ohio. 1880.
HOFSTADTER, RICHARD, and Wilson Smith, eds., *American Higher Education: A Documentary History*. Chicago, 1961.
HOPKINS, ALPHONSO A., *The Life of Clinton Bowen Fisk*. New York: Negro Universities Press, 1969; first pub. 1888.
HOWARD, WARREN S., *American Slavers and the Federal Law, 1837-1862*. Berkeley, 1963.
LARIMER, DORENE HEACOCK, "Evaluation of John Ogden–Educator," B.A. Thesis, Pacific College [George Fox College], Newberg, Oregon, 1933.
LOVE, WILLIAM DELOSS, *Wisconsin in the War of the Rebellion: A History of all Regiments and Batteries*. Chicago, 1866.
MACMULLEN, EDITH NYE, *In the Cause of True Education: Henry Barnard and Nineteenth-Century School Reform*. New Haven: Yale University Press, 1991.
MCCLENDON, CARLEE T., *Edgefield Marriage Records: Edgefield , SC*. Columbia, SC, 1970.
MCGHEE, C. STUART, "E. O. Tade, Freedmen's Education, and the Failure of Reconstruction in Tennessee," *Tennessee Historical Quarterly* 43 (Winter, 1984): 376-389.
MCPHERSON, JAMES M. *The Abolitionist Legacy: From Reconstruction to the NAACP*. Princeton: Princeton University Press, 1975.
———, *Struggle for Equality: Abolitionists and the Negro in the Civil War and Reconstruction*. Princeton: Princeton University Press, 1964.
———, "White Liberals and Black Power in Negro Education, 1865-1915," *American Historical Review*, 75 (June 1970).
MARSH, J. B. T., *The Story of the Jubilee Singers*. Boston, 1880.
MERRIAM, LUCIUS S., *Higher Education in Tennessee*. Washington, DC, 1893.
MIKESELL, THOMAS, *The County of Fulton* [Ohio]. Madison, Wisconsin, 1905.
MORRIS, ROBERT C., *Reading, 'Riting, and Reconstruction: The Education of Freedmen in the South, 1861-1970*. Chicago, 1981).
MORROW, RALPH E., *Northern Methodism and Reconstruction*. East Lansing, 1956.
Nashville Daily Gazette
Nashville Daily Press and Times
Nashville Daily Union
Nashville Dispatch
Nashville Republican Banner
OGDEN, JOHN, *Outlines of a Complete System of Pedagogical Science, Prepared for the use of Normal Schools, Normal Classes, Teachers' Institutes, and Private Learners*. Columbus, 1878.
———, *The Science of Education and Art of Teaching*. Cincinnati, 1859.
PARSONS, MIRA CLARKE, "Historic Worthington," *Ohio Archaeological and Historical Publications*, 13 (1904), 71-82.
PATTON, JAMES WELCH, *Unionism and Reconstruction in Tennessee, 1860-1869*. Chapel Hill, 1934.

PEARSON, ELIZABETH W., ed., *Letters from Port Royal Written at the Time of the Civil War*. New York, 1969; first pub. 1906.

PHILLIPS, PAUL DAVID, "A History of the Freedmen's Bureau in Tennessee," Ph.D. diss., Vanderbilt University, 1964.

QUINER, E. B., *The Military History of Wisconsin: A Record of the Civil and Military Patriotism of the State in the War for the Union*. Chicago, 1866.

RABINOWITZ, HOWARD N., "Half a Loaf: The Shift from White to Black Teachers in the Negro Schools of the Urban South, 1865-1900," *Journal of Southern History*, 40:4 (Nov. 1974).

REIGHARD, FRANK, *A Standard History of Fulton County, Ohio*. New York, 1920.

RICHARDSON, JOE, *Christian Reconstruction: The American Missionary Association and Southern Blacks, 1861-1890*. Athens, GA: University of Georgia Press, 1986.

———, "Fisk University: The First Critical Years, " *Tennessee Historical Quarterly* 29:1 (1970).

———, *A History of Fisk University, 1865-1946*. University, AL: University of Alabama Press, 1980.

RÖBERT, CHARLES, E., *Nashville and Her Trade for 1870*. Nashville, 1870.

ROWELL, JOHN W., *Yankee Cavalrymen: Through the Civil War with the Ninth Pennsylvania Cavalry*. Knoxville, 1971.

SWINT, HENRY L., *Northern Teacher in the South, 1862-1870*. Nashville, 1941.

———, "Notes and Comments: Reports from Educational Agents of the Freedmen's Bureau in Tennessee, 1865-1870," *Tennessee Historical Quarterly*, 1 (March-December 1942).

TALBOT, JEAN, "The First State Normal School, 1860: Winona State College, 1960, " *Quarterly Bulletin of Winona State College*, 1959-1960.

TAYLOR, ALRUTHEUS A., Fisk University and the Nashville Community, 1866-1900," *Journal of Negro History* , 39:2 (April, 1954).

TURNER, JAMES, *Without God, Without Creed: The Origins of Unbelief in America*. Baltimore: Johns Hopkins University Press, 1985.

VAUGHN, WILLIAM B., *Schools for All: The Blacks and Public Education in the South, 1865-1877*. Lexington, 1974.

WELLS, TOM H., *Slave Ship Wanderer*. Athens: University of Georgia Press, 1967.

Westland Educator. Lisbon, ND, Sept. 1910.

WHEELER, WILLIAM OGDEN, *The Ogden Family in America*. Philadelphia, 1907.

WISHEK, NINA FARLEY, *Along the Trails of Yesterday: The Story of McIntosh County* [North Dakota]. Froh, Pohl, and Monch, ND: The Ashley Tribune, 1940.

WOODROW GUILD of the First Presbyterian Church, *Shedding Light on Worthington*, 2nd ed. Worthington, OH, 1953.

INDEX

Abolitionism 6, 23
Abolitionist legacy 1-3
Aid societies 26, 46, 77
    See also Freedmen's aid societies
Alabama, Stevenson 14
Allen, Alice A. 52
Allen, Rev. R.H. 36, 38
Alvord, John
    Freedmen's Bureau Education
    Superintendent 80
American Missionary Association
    (AMA) 1, 25, 29, 31, 34-36, 40, 42, 46-47,
    56, 57, 59, 75-77
    and normal schools 46-47
Annapolis, Maryland 24
Appleby, Miss Addie
    Fisk School faculty 75
Aray, Mrs. L.E.
    Fisk School faculty 52, 75
Arcana Lodge #272, Crestline, Ohio 22
Atlanta, Georgia
    Campaign 16
    Negro education in 27
Augusta, Georgia 16

Bailey, Gamaliel 6
Barnard, Henry 6
Bedford, Ohio
    Fisk faculty from 75
Beech Grove, South Carolina 20
Benedict, Miss Julia E.
    Fisk School faculty 75
Bennett, Rev. H.S. 52, 59-60, 75
Bismarck, North Dakota 93, 94
    Ogdens reside in 92
Board of Education
    Nashville, Tennessee 73
Bosson, Senator William, of Tennessee 36, 64
bowels, Inflammation of 14
Boynton, Dr. 72
Brewster, Anna Augusta xi, 10, 25, 52, 54, 56,
    59, 61-62, 74-75, 82, 91
    becomes main breadwinner 90
    as kindergartner 91, 93
    at Tennessee State Teachers' Association
        meeting 64
    as kindergartner 77, 87, 90
    death of 94
    personality of 75
Brooks, Mr. and Mrs. David
    Edgefield, South Carolina 22
Brown, Mr.
    of Rutherford county, Tennessee 66
Brownlow, Governor William G., of
    Tennessee 35-39
Brunson, Mr.
    Captor, near Edgefield, S.C. 22
Brunswick, Georgia 19
Buchanan, President James 63
Bull Run, First Battle of 9
Bureau of Refugees, Freedmen, and
    Abandoned Lands--see Freedmen's
    Bureau
Burnt Hickory, Georgia 16, 19
Burrows, John H. 53
Burt, Rev. David 45, 64, 66
    Freedmen's Bureau School
    Superintendent in Tennessee 45

Camp Sorghum
Columbia, South Carolina 16
Cape Girardeau, Missouri 13, 94
Carter, George W., Confederate officer 13
Chapel
    at Fisk School 56
Charleston, South Carolina
    Confederate prison in 16
Charlotte, North Carolina 23
Chattanooga Depot
    Nashville, Tennessee 32, 39-40
Chattanooga, Tennessee 15, 27, 53, 73
Chickamauga, Georgia
    Battle of 15
Christian morality
    taught at Fisk School 68-70
Cincinnati, Ohio 1, 6, 25, 42
    Fisk faculty from 75
Clapp, Ada 59
Cleveland, Ohio 73-74, 83
    establishment of kindergartens in 77
    National Education Association
        meets in 73
Coffin, Levi 1, 26
Colamer, Ohio
    Fisk faculty from 75
Cole, Annetta (Mrs. William W.
    Goodman) 22
Colored Infantry Band
    15th U. S. 36
Colored schools 64

Colored Tennessean, Nashville
    newspaper 39
Columbia, South Carolina 17
Confederate prison camp in 16, 23
Columbus, Ohio x, 4, 24, 93
    establishment of kindergartens in 77
Conatty, Thomas J., Capt., First
    Wisconsin Cavalry 11
Confederate prison
    Ogden in 16
Congregational Church 55-59
Cowan, Miss L.A.
    Fisk School faculty 75
Cravath, Erastus M. 1, 30-33, 36, 38-39, 42,
    45, 61, 84
Cravath, Mrs. Erastus M. 34
Crawfordsville, Indiana
    Fisk faculty from 75
Crestline, Ohio x, 3, 14
    Arcana Lodge #272 23
Crosby, Charles 59
Cumberland, Dept. of, Signal Corps
    Officer Examination Board 13-14
Curse of Cain 63
Curse of Ham 63

Daily Press and Times, Nashville,
    Tennessee 44
Dakota Territory 91
Dakota Territory, McIntosh county 91
Daniels, Colonel Edward, First Wisconsin
    Cavalry 11
Decorah, Iowa
    Fisk faculty from 75
Delaware, Ohio 4
Department of the Cumberland 13
    Signal Corps Examination Board 13-14
depression
    of 1873 48
diarrhea 14
discriminatory poll tax
    introduced in Tennessee 81
dogs
    role in capture 22
Doughty, Mr.
    member, Tennessee House of
    Representatives 67
Douglass, Miss E.W.
    Fisk School faculty 75
DuBois, W.E.B.
    student at Fisk University 69
Dunbar, Barney 19
    plantation of 20, 22

Easter, Miss E.A. 40
economic development for Freedmen 25
Edgefield, South Carolina 16, 22, 23
    Yankees in, during Civil War 23
education, as profession 77
education for Freedmen 24, 26
    diminishing enthusiasm for 78
education, public
    hostility to in Tennessee 82
educators
    in Civil War 12
Elizabeth Peabody Kindergarten Training
    School
    Minneapolis, Minnesota 93
Episcopal Church 61
Ewers, E.P.
    Fayette Normal, Music, and Business
    College 90
exhaustion when at Fisk
    Ogden reveals 84

family
    as reason for resignation from Fisk 76-77
Fayette Normal, Music, and Business
    College
    Fayette, Ohio xi, 90
Fifteenth Iowa Infantry 16
Fifteenth U. S. Colored Infantry Band 36
fights
    between White and Black boys in
    Nashville 41
First Wisconsin Cavalry x, 11-15
Fisk School 2, 25, 38, 39
    as college 39
    as normal school 39, 47, 49-50, 64,
    71-72
    Board of Trustees 29, 48-49
    description of 36
    faculty 75
    faculty attitudes toward Ogden 83
    founding of 30-32, 34
    invites Ogden to fortieth anniversary
    celebration 94
    John Ogden, Principal of 30, 42
    opening exercises 35-40
    physical condition of 41, 78
    Principalship, job description
    for 42-43
    student letters 51-53
    university status 48-50, 76
Fisk University–See Fisk School
Fisk, General Clinton B. 27-28, 32-34, 36-38,
    40-43, 84

continues to support Fisk School 44
Freedmen's Bureau Assistant Commissioner
   for Tenn. and Kentucky 28
   leaves Nashville 44
free labor 25
Freedmen's aid societies 24, 46
   diminishing monetary support from 78
Freedmen's Bureau x, 3, 25, 28-29
   in Kentucky 24-25, 27-28
   in Tennessee 24-25, 27-28
Freedmen's Bureau school superintendency
   in Tennessee 42, 44-45
Freedmen's Bureau, General Superintendent
   of Schools 80
Fulton County, Ohio 90

Gambier, Ohio
   Kenyon College xi, 73, 83, 86-87
Garfield Kindergarten
   Washington, D.C. 90
Garland, Mary J.
   and Froebel method 77
Garrison, William Lloyd 3
Georgia, Augusta 16, 19
Georgia, Brunswick 19
Georgia, Burnt Hickory 16, 19
Georgia, Macon 27
Georgia, Marietta 16
Georgia, Savannah 16
God, existence of 18
   taught at Fisk School 68-69
Goodman, Mr. and Mrs. William W.
   of Edgefield, South Carolina 23
gossip vii
Grand Army of the Republic 91
   North Dakota 92
Granny
   on Barney Dunbar's Plantation 20

Ham, curse of 63
Hamburg, South Carolina 22
harangue
   Ogden accused of delivering 64-65
Hardtack 14
Harris, Rev. Mr. 38
Hawkins, Augustus 54
Hayden, Miss Sarah L.
   Fisk School faculty 75
health of John Ogden
   in Army Service 14-15
hemorrhoids 14
Herald and Philanthropist, abolitionist
   newspaper 6

Hopedale, Ohio 4
Horse Creek, South Carolina 20
Howard Chapel
   at Fisk School 55-56
Howard, General O.O. 43-44
Hunt, Fred 52
Hyden, Rev.
   of McMinn county, Tennessee 67

Institute Work
   proposed for American West 91
integrated schools 64
   impossibility of 66
   Ogden favors 71
Iowa, Fifteenth Infantry 16

jail, Edgefield, South Carolina 16
Johnson, President Andrew 43-44, 82
Jubilee Singers 78
   on first tour in Ohio 84-85

Kansas
   First Wisconsin Cavalry in 12
Kentucky 27-28, 42
Kentucky, Covington
   Freedmen's Bureau schools in 42
Kentucky, Cynthiana
   Freedmen's Bureau Schools in 42
Kenyon College xi, 83, 86
   Gambier, Ohio 73
Kenyon Grammar School
   preparatory school of Kenyon College
   86
Kindergarten movement 77, 87
Kindergarten Training School
   Washington, D.C. 90
Kirkpatrick, Lt. George W., 15th Iowa
   Infantry 16-17
Ku Klux Klan 82
   founded in Tennessee 81

LaGrange, Colonel Oscar H.
   Commander, First Wisconsin
   Cavalry 94
Lakeview Cemetery, Seattle, Washington
   Ogden buried in 94
Lamar, Charles Augustus Lafayette, Confederate officer 19
Lamar, Thomas Gresham, Confederate
   officer 19
Latin, teaching of 72, 76
levity
   in church matters 62

Index

Lewis, M.H.
    at Ohio Central Normal School 87
Lindsley, J. B., Nashville School
    Superintendent 36
Loudon, Tennessee 14

Macon, Georgia 27
    Confederate prison in 16
Madisonville, Tennessee 14
Maginness, Julia A.
    Fisk School faculty 75
Mansfield, Ohio x
Marietta, Georgia 16
Marmaduke, Confederate General 12
Martha's Vineyard Summer Institute 91
Maryland Parole Camp 24
Maryland, Annapolis 24
Mason, Thomas 51
Masonic affiliation of John Ogden 18, 22
Masons 18
master's degree 4
McIntosh County, Dakota Territory xi, 91
McKee, Rev. J.G. 31-32, 41
    opposes integrated schools 66-67
McNeely Normal School, Hopedale,
    Ohio x, 4
McPherson, James M., historian 1-3, 11
Mears, Subagent for Maury county,
    Tennessee 45
Methodist Church vii, 6, 55, 59
Mills, Judge 66
Milnor Hall
    preparatory school at Kenyon
    College 86-87
Milnor State Normal School xi
    North Dakota 91
Milnor, North Dakota xi, 91
Minneapolis, Minnesota
    Ogdens move to 93
Minnesota Education Association
    Ogden made life member of 94
Minnesota State Normal School,
    Winona 7-9, 46
    Ogden resigns principalship of 9
Minnesota, St. Paul 25, 91
Minnesota, Winona 7, 9, 45-46
Missouri
    Cape Girardeau 12
    First Wisconsin Cavalry in 12-14
Missouri State Militia 12
Mitchell, Mary Jane x, 7, 89
Mitchell, William
    Ohio Superintendent of Public
    Instruction 87
Model School
    at Fisk School 71
Morgan, Miss Helen C. 55
    Fisk School faculty 55, 75
Mount Vernon, Ohio x, 3
Mullery, Brother 54
Muster out of Union Army
    Columbus, Ohio 24

Nashville Board of Education 72-73
Nashville Daily Gazette 40
Nashville *Daily Press and Times* 35
Nashville Daily Union 39
Nashville Republican Banner 64
Nashville, Tennessee 31, 48
    newspapers 34-35, 39
    Ogdens depart from 74
National Education Association
    annual meeting, 1870 70
    Normal School Division 73
    Ogden as president of Normal
    School Division 73
National Era, abolitionist newspaper 6
Negro district
    Nashville, Tennessee 32
Negro recruiting 13
    in Georgia 16
    in Tennessee 13
Negroes
    African born 20, 21
New York Yacht Club 19
Normal-school question 46, 48, 71
Normal-school teaching function
    Ogden continues 86
North Dakota 91
    Ogdens depart from 92
North Dakota, Milnor 91
North Dakota, Sargent county 91

Oberlin, Ohio
    Fisk faculty from 75
Officer's Military Hospital
    Chattanooga, Tennessee 15
Ogden, Arthur 77
Ogden, Clara Landon 10, 88, 93
    wedding of 89
Ogden, Helen Augusta 88
Ogden, John v, 34, 62
    accused of being lukewarm Christian
    55-56
    appears to be at end of professional
    life 90

cautiousness about Negro education 62
Civil War service 10-23
in Columbus, Ohio 23, 26, 28
dentures 14
education of 3-4
educational ideas of 9
favors racially integrated schools 63-65, 70-71
health of, in Army 14-16
leaves limelight 74
mild treatment of, by Southerners 82
Negro regiment recruiting 14
as Normal School Principal 4, 7-9
North Dakota Superintendent of Public Instruction 91
said not to be a gentleman 54
not antagonistic to Southerners 45
not sectarian 61-62
obituary of 94
only threat made to in Nashville 82
poetry of 7, 9, 15
accused of having a poor moral reputation 54
praised as a noble fellow 94
president of Normal School Division, National Education Assn. 73
psychological state of at Fisk School 84
publications 4
reasons for leaving Fisk School 75
salary of 29-30, 34, 43
scholarly and professional writing 87
science of Education and the Art of Teaching 68
Signal Corps Examination Board, service on 13
Superintendent of Education, Freedmen's Bureau 28-30, 42
Superintendent of Fisk School 29, 42
Superintendent of Schools for Freedmen's Bureau 28-30, 42
sympathy for Negroes 62
Western Freedmen's Aid Commission, agent for 26-28, 30, 42
Ogden, John, Jr. 52, 76
Ogden, Mrs. John (first wife)--see Mitchell, Mary Jane
Ogden, Mrs. John (second wife)--see Brewster, Anna Augusta
Ohio Central Normal and Kindergarten Training School 87
Ohio Central Normal School, Worthington, Ohio xi, 85, 87
as business venture 89
Ogden becomes co-proprietor of 85
Ohio Wesleyan University x, 3-4, 69
Ohio, Cleveland 74
Ohio, Columbus 93
Ohio, Crestline x, 3, 14
Ohio, Fayette 90
Ohio, Galion 88
Ohio, Gambier 83
Kenyon College 73
Ohio, Hopedale 4
Ohio, Mount Vernon 3
Ohio, Worthington 85
"Outlines of a Complete System of Pedagogical Science," by John Ogden xi, 88
Owen, John A., Lt., First Wisconsin Cavalry 12

Paley, William
author of *Natural Theology*, 1802 69
Peabody Education Fund 48, 55, 67, 72
supports Fisk School 67
Peabody, Elizabeth P.
and Froebel method 77
poll tax, discriminatory
introduced in Tennessee 81
prejudices of the people 66
Preparatory Department of Kenyon College
Ogden as principal of 73
Presbyterian Church 61
Presbyterian Board of Missions 31
Professionalization in teaching 8, 77
public school law, Tennessee 80

racially integrated schools 64
racially separate schools
high cost of 65
Racine, Wisconsin 12
radical
Ogden accused of being 64
Rebel Hospital
Columbia, South Carolina 16
Reconstruction 26
in Tennessee 80
violence 81
Red Wing, Minnesota 11
redemption
in Tennessee 82
relief
for Freedmen 26

Index

Ripon, Wisconsin 94
Richardson, Joe, historian 74, 85
Robinson, Mrs. M.J.
   Fisk School faculty 75
Robinson, Rev. 66
role models
   freedmen lacking 79
Rust, Rev. R. S. 30, 32, 43
Rutting, Thomas
   student at Fisk School 68

Sambo 39
Sargent County, North Dakota xi, 91
Savannah River 16, 20
Sawyer, M. 43
schools, common
   Ogden says intrinsically democratic 64
Science of Education and the Art of Teaching, by John Ogden 4, 68, 88
Sears, Dr. Barnabas, of Peabody
   Education Fund 48, 67, 71-72
   praises Fisk School 83
Seattle, Washington xi, 94
secession 9
secessionsville, Battle of
   referred to 19
segregated schools
   Ogden opposes 63, 64
segregation
   legalized in Tennessee 81
Semple, Miss Carrie M. 58
   Fisk School faculty 58, 75
sentimentality
   in Ogden's poetry 15
Sheppard, Miss Ella
   Fisk School faculty 75
Sherman, Gen. William T.
   March to the Sea of 20
Shipman, S.V., Capt., First Wisconsin
   Cavalry 12-13
Signal Corps Examination Board 13-14
skirmish
   at Whitewater River, Missouri 13
Slave ship *Wanderer* 19, 21
slavery 9
slaves, fugitive
   in Georgia 16
slaves, Ogden's gratitude to 23
Smith, Edward Parmelee 1-3, 30-32, 34, 43, 53, 56, 62, 83
   complains to Ogden 76
social equality
   Southerners fear of 81

South
   Ogden claims limited intelligence in 64
South Carolina x, 15
South Carolina, Beech Grove 20
South Carolina,
   Charleston 16
   Columbia 16
   Edgefield, jail in 16, 22
   Hamburg 22
   Horse Creek 20
Spence, Adam K. 45, 75, 83
St. Andrew Sound, Georgia 19
St. John's Protestant Episcopal Church
   Worthington, Ohio 88
St. Louis, Missouri
   John Ogden in 14
St. Paul, Minnesota 25, 91
Stevenson, Alabama 14
Stewart, Donald Ogden 88
Stewart, Judge Gilbert Holland 89, 93
Stewart, Mrs. Gilbert Holland--see
   Ogden, Clara Landon
Stratton, Miss L. Mina
   Fisk School faculty 75
Strieby, Rev. Michael, of the AMA
   1, 59, 60, 76
students
   of Minnesota State Normal School in Civil War 12, 25
Superintendent of Public Instruction
   North Dakota xi, 92
Superintendent of Schools, Freedmen's Bureau
   John Alvord 80
Swallow, Hannah M. 59
Swint, Henry L., Tennessee
   Reconstruction historian 80

Tade, E.O. 2, 53-55
Teachers' institutes 6
   in Tennessee 70
teaching, as profession 9, 77
   fringe benefits sought in 77
Tennessee 48-49
   as reactionary state 81
   despondency in, 1870 80
   First Wisconsin Cavalry in 13-15
   Ku Klux Klan founded in 81
   Negro regiment recruiting in 14
   Reconstruction in 80
   segregation, first state to legalize 81
   state government of 47-48

Tennessee legislature
    repeals state public education law 82
Tennessee public school law 80
Tennessee State Teachers' Association 67
    Annual meeting, Nashville, 1867 64
Tennessee, Chattanooga 15, 53, 73
Tennessee, common school system of
    Ogden calls progressive and
    democratic 65
Tennessee, Eastern
    Civil War in 14
Tennessee, Knoxville 70
Tennessee, Memphis 51-52, 82
Tennessee, Mt. Pleasant 45
Tennessee, Murfreesboro 52
Tennessee, Nashville 31, 82
Tennessee, Shelbyville 70
Tennessee, Woodbury 52
Thirteenth Wisconsin Infantry 14
thirst, as prison escapee 17
Trenton, New Jersey 73
Tyler, President John 63

Union Army Construction Corps
    Hospital
    Nashville, Tennessee 32
Union church 56-61
Unionville, Ohio
    Fisk faculty from 75
United Presbyterian Board of Missions to
    the Freedmen 31

visionary
    Ogden accused of being 64

Walden, Rev. J.M. 28, 31
    Western Freedmen's Aid
    Commission 26
Wanderer, slave ship, 1858 19, 21-22
Washington, D.C. xi, 6, 24
    Anna Augusta Brewster moves to 90
    Ogdens depart from 91

Washington, Seattle
    Ogdens move to 94
Western Freedmen's Aid Commission
    (WFAC) 1- 3, 25-31, 34-36, 42, 57
    merges into AMA, 1870 76
Westland Educator, Lisbon, North
    Dakota 94
Whipple, Rev. George, of AMA 47, 71,
    75
White, George L. 52, 59, 75
    Ogden corresponds with 83-84
White, Laura C. 59
White, Mercilia 59
Whitewater River, Missouri, skirmish
    at 12-13
Williams, Mr.
    member, Tennessee House of
    Representatives 67
Wilmington, North Carolina 23
Winona, Minnesota x, 7, 11, 12, 45, 54
Wisconsin 6, 7, 91
    education in 7
Wisconsin Normal School Board of
    Regents 7, 11
Wisconsin, Kenosha 12
Wisconsin, Madison 91
Wisconsin, Milwaukee 12
Wisconsin, Racine 12
Wisconsin, Ripon 94
Woodbury, Connecticut
    Fisk faculty from 75
Worthington, Ohio xi, 84-85, 88, 89
    Ogdens depart from 89

Yankee civilians
    in South Carolina during Civil War 23
Yankee teachers 81
    Southern dislike of 81
Young, Rev. Charles, A.M.
    Worthington, Ohio 88

www.ingramcontent.com/pod-product-compliance
Lightning Source LLC
Chambersburg PA
CBHW080801020526
44114CB00035B/2